EXECUTIVE JOB SEARCH STRATEGIES

Robert C. Bruce

VGM Career Horizons
a division of *NTC Publishing Group*
Lincolnwood, Illinois USA

To my wife Gloria, who for 20 years encouraged me to write
this book.

As usual there are a number of important people who helped
bring this book into existence. Without their work and encouragement, it would still just be in my head. A particular thanks to
Charlene Kile, who typed many draft revisions and the final manuscript. Also, to Jo Anne Cripe, Kerry Barnet-Martin, and Diana
Dobbins Seder who provided editing suggestions, and to NTC
Publishing Group, for bringing the book to life.

Library of Congress Cataloging-in-Publication Data

Bruce, Robert C.
    Executive job search strategies : the guide to career transitions
/ Robert C. Bruce.
        p.   cm.
    Includes bibliographical references.
    ISBN 0-8442-4375-2
    1. Career changes—United States.   2. Executives—United States.
3. Job hunting—United States.   I. Title.
HF5384.B78   1994
650.14'024'658—dc20   93-47508
                                                     CIP

Published by VGM Career Horizons, a division of NTC Publishing Group
4255 West Touhy Avenue
Lincolnwood (Chicago), Illinois 60646–1975, U.S.A.

4 5 6 7 8 9 0 VP 9 8 7 6 5 4 3 2 1

Contents

Introduction

Why This Book?

During the 1980s and into the 1990s more than 10 million people were released from their jobs. Of these, 12 to 14 percent are executives, leaving major organizations. For the most part, these executives are highly paid and older, but not ready to retire. What happens to them? How do they cope with the mid-life crisis that sudden job loss throws them into?

If you are a victim of downsizing, this book will show you how to get your career—and your life—back on track. If you are still employed but are threatened by future layoff, or you simply feel it's time to make a switch to a new job or a new career field, this book will help you make the most of your options.

You will learn to develop a positive plan of action and generate a new career direction.

Yesterday is a canceled check.
Tomorrow is a promissory note.
Today is ready cash...use it.

CHAPTER 1

Middle Manager's Crisis

A Sign of the Times

If one word could characterize the employment climate of the 1990s, that word would be "change." Whether it's the composition of the workforce, downsizing, rightsizing, or the elimination of middle managers, nothing is the same as it was yesterday. It's as if we have sailed for years on familiar waters, only to find we have passed into a new and uncharted sea. The sea we have entered holds the potential for new rewards, but it is fraught with danger.

In an attempt to manage change in these turbulent times, we must anticipate it. If there has been a single phenomenon that has affected the working force in America, it is the downsizing that has been going on for the past ten years. Almost every industry has been hit with downsizing. A closer look at some of the specifics shows the impact this has had on today's job market. While the economy is growing steadily again, more than 9 million Americans—more than 7 percent of the workforce—remain jobless, victims of changes they cannot control.

According to the Bureau of Labor Statistics (BLS), more than 6 million people are working part-time because they can't find a full-time job. Another million or so have simply given up looking for work. This means nearly 17 million people, or almost 12% of the labor force, are unemployed or underemployed.

BusinessWeek estimates that more than a million managers and staff professionals lost their jobs during the decade of the 1980s. That trend has continued into the 1990s. One half of all the lay-offs of the *BusinessWeek* study was equally divided among supervisors, middle managers, senior managers, technicians, and non-managerial professionals. So, if you have recently been subject to the effects of downsizing, you are not alone.

Drake Beam Morin, a major outplacement firm, has seen its business mushroom as middle managers are displaced. The outplacement business, which was hardly known seven years ago, has grown to a $500 million-plus business. According to DBM, the average search takes a month longer than it did last year and about 38% of the clients accept jobs at a lower salary when they do find new employment. These people are working their way down the career ladder, working at jobs and pay levels they experienced five to ten years before. But many are happy just to be gainfully em-ployed, producing and contributing again.

Not surprisingly, the unemployment rate for managers and pro-fessionals is very difficult to assess accurately. The blue-collar worker, when laid off, goes home and waits for resolution. In a few days or weeks, something shows up again or a call back from the union comes through. Whereas the blue collar working situa-tion is fluid and fast changing, the white collar worker sits on an iceberg in an ocean. Those who are reported through the Bureau of Labor Statistics are only those who are drawing unemployment for an allotted time. Statistics do not include those who are under-employed, or those who are no longer eligible for unemployment insurance, those who have too much pride to collect unemploy-ment checks or those who are in hiding under the guise of consul-tants. According to another outplacement organization, Right Associates, more than 15% of a sample of recent clients ended up self-employed. What this doesn't say is whether these people join the entrepreneurial ranks because they want to or because they have to. Are they going into their small business because it's a stopgap until the real job comes along or is it a permanent plan being brought about by the economic times? Generalizations are difficult at best, as management-level job changers may be looking for an appropriate new career, consulting, or opening a small cottage business all at the same time.

Age and Salary Considerations

Clearly, the growing trend is toward a thinly veiled form of age and salary discrimination. And it has been going on for at least ten years. At first, it was slow, as employers waited to see if there were going to be legal suits. Although the lower courts are filled with discrimination suits, few cases have reached the higher courts.

Many of the people being released today are older, more highly paid executives usually in their mid-forties or fifties, pulling down major paychecks frequently near or in the six figure range. Typically an organization will lay off three executives and replace them with two junior people or graduates fresh out of college. Those two new people will be expected to work harder and produce more than the outgoing three had to in the last ten years. And even that scenario is changing as corporations are getting rid of those over-50, $100,000 executives and replacing them with college graduates who are half their age and earning a third of their salary.

What is being surplused is the talent that made the American corporation the world leader over the past few decades.

A Conference Board survey of 400 major corporations found about 40 percent of the firms surveyed offered packages to early retirees as a part of downsizing efforts. The Conference Board study found that companies continue to lay off and package out senior managers even though they are more reliable than younger employees, have better work attitudes, have better job skills, are absent less often, and are less likely to quit. About 70 percent of the companies surveyed also said older workers were at least as cost effective as their younger colleagues.

Hiring them makes good business sense. However, the report went on to say that job hunters are more likely to be successful if they are prepared to relocate, retrain, and accept lower pay.

But the truth is more complex. Although older people's cognitive skills are slower, they compensate with improved judgment, experience, and wisdom and thus perform equally well. Other images are also wrong. Rather than being depressed, older workers score higher than their juniors in job satisfaction surveys. The "Young and the Restless" is more than a television show.

Another stereotype comes about as a result of youthful personnel department representatives who interview older applicants. Perhaps unconsciously these employer representatives view the applicants as parental figures and shy away from hiring them.

The Part-Time Phenomenon

An additional phenomenon is taking place and that is the trend toward part-time positions. More than 90 percent of the 365,000 jobs created by U.S. companies in 1993 were part-time positions. Already one in three U.S. workers has joined this working army. None of these people have job security, and they usually have no benefits.

The concept is for a company to identify its basic employees; non-core activities can then be done by peripheral workers, part-timers, or sub-contractors. Company loyalty is a thing of the past. Because of the speed of change, it's in no one's interest to make commitments. Disposable workers can be hired or released. When business is good, you gear up. As soon as there is a lull, you discard your part-timers. Admittedly, you pay a premium for these workers if you hire them through an agency, but not necessarily if you hire directly. From the company perspective the benefits are that it does not have to pay a 38 percent cost for fringe benefits, it has reduced liability in unemployment claims and workers compensation, and it will never be stuck with someone who is not working out.

How does that affect the executive? Well, for many executives it can be very attractive. It can mean being hired by your old employer or another employer in your field as an independent contractor or consultant. You get to work, be productive, and avoid the stress and frustration of long hours. You can make your contribution then move on to something different. Once you get a reputation, work will find you.

In many respects, part-time assignments can be the executive's ideal situation. They avoid the long stressful hours of full-time employment, keep you involved, and keep your brain cells active. You may work hard during the project but it does have an ending.

I was once involved with two executives who began a "Rent-An-Executive" firm. Their name described their activities. Another executive was successfully working with a consulting firm on a temporary basis. When the consulting firm had a client and need for his expertise, it would call.

In many respects the part-time phenomenon plays well for the executive and should not be overlooked. Temporary work can be a preview for full-time employment. The organization gets to look at you, you get to evaluate the employer, and down the road it may end in a permanent arrangement. How many of us have hired full-time the part-time secretary we had a chance to evaluate?

The Hidden Job Market

Many trends in the latter part of the 1990s will depend upon the economic recovery package. It has been estimated that job growth has got to come from the small to medium-size employers: Fortune 1000 firms are downsizing. If the country's infrastructure is rebuilt by the small and medium-size companies, then the future will look bright for the surplused executive. The small unknown company will go to its local bank and get funding for stronger capitalization, expansion of facilities, and new research and development. In turn, the expansion will need experienced, talented executives who can step in and immediately make a difference. The smaller companies will not be inclined to train or look for long-term solutions. They will need proven talent that can accept responsibility to help the next phase of the organization. If and when this happens, there will be a stable full of highly qualified executives ready to step in and use their expertise. The secret of the outplaced professional is this so-called "hidden job market."

Why is it "hidden?" Because these small to mid-size employers do not have sophisticated personnel departments, they do not recruit on campus, they do not have formal training programs, and they do not advertise openings in major newspapers. Frequently, they are unclear as to job duties and responsibilities and are ignorant on the going pay rate. If approached correctly, executives can engineer their own job, pay, and responsibilities.

In essence, these companies are invisible in their hiring process. And they want new managers to become productive immediately.

There is also a trend, though in much smaller numbers, toward new alliances being forged by small groups of outplaced people gathering together in basements and garages to create the next-generation of start-up companies.

When to Make the Move

Today you develop a set of transferable skills that you carry from employer to employer (your tool kit) and you must be productive up to the day you draw your last paycheck. If not, you could be gone.

In light of the tight job market, the question is "Should I switch employers if things are stagnant with my present situation?" If you see your boss is still young and promotions are few and far between, that is a judgment call that you need to make. In some cases the organization gives you strokes indicating you are one of the chosen but there just isn't anyplace to go right now. Rather than get impatient and go elsewhere, you might do better in the long run if you stay put and wait for things to open up where you are. However, there are always situations where sitting and waiting will produce nothing.

You read the situation as going nowhere and so you dust off the resume, update it, and begin timidly to venture into the job market, being very careful not to let your present employer know your intentions. The problem is that busy people often don't have the energy left over to conduct the job search. Many people do the mental job search while stuck in traffic on the freeway. However, they are top performers who put in long hours and find very little time or energy left over to conduct a proper campaign. The temptation is to quit the job so they can devote full time to a job search. But that is absolutely a mistake in today's business climate. Never quit a job to look for a job.

You might decide to stick with your present career. Most people I deal with do end up taking jobs that are similar to their previous positions. Many terminations are caused by factors that are not connected to performance problems, cutbacks, or chemistry issues. If you possess and enjoy using the skills that your last job demanded, performing the same work in a new environment may solve your career dilemma.

If you are determined you are going to make a change, you need to use all the tools and resources available to you. You need to develop a chart to establish a full game plan of what you are going to do on a daily basis. To succeed at this process, you must catalog and organize your resources, target your search, and plan your campaign.

Only after you come to grips with the fact that the average search takes six to nine months, and prepare yourself psychologically and financially, do you begin to cope with your situation and start the long, hard, and often discouraging task of conducting the job search. Work is therapeutic. It plays a major role in our sense of self and well being. The goal is to identify the work for which you are most qualified and that you most enjoy, then diligently and systematically seek it out.

Benjamin Franklin expressed it well when he said, "When men are employed, they are best contented; for on the days they worked they were good natured and cheerful, and, with the consciousness of having done a good day's work, they spent the evening joyously; but on idle days they were mutinous and quarrelsome."

Many people do not plan. In a rush to hit the ground running, they neglect to choose a destination, or even a direction, before they begin their travels. Getting a job as quickly as possible becomes the single goal of the job search. Planning doesn't play a role in the campaign.

Searching for work should be a systematic process. The people who stick to that process find careers. No matter how intelligent, experienced, or energetic they may be, the individuals who either do not make or stay with their plans have the most trouble finding careers.

For those people who have a plan and are diligent in applying that plan and recognizing the time frame required to get a job in the 1990s, and apply the principles set forth in the remaining part of this book, there will be exciting opportunities ahead. There are good jobs out there even in the worst recession in thirty years. The future looks bright.

The Bureau of Labor Statistics offers optimistic projections for job growth between 1990 and 2005. During that period, 24.6 million jobs will be created and there will be a 20 percent growth in employment. Although that's about half the growth rate of the previous fifteen year period, the difference results not from any weakening of America's capacity to create jobs but almost entirely from much slower growth of the labor force. Service industries will create virtually all the new jobs, with manufacturing falling by 600,000, assuming moderate growth during the period.

As in the recent past, job growth will be the fastest in highly skilled, highly paid occupations, the BLS predicts. Executives, managers, professionals, and technicians, a quarter of today's workers, will account for 41 percent of all job growth until 2005, with managerial jobs in marketing, public relations, advertising, communications, engineering, and labor relations proliferating at a fast clip. Among professional jobs, those for computer analysts, psychologists, health professionals, and lawyers are predicted to grow most quickly.

It has been my experience that although people who have been downsized would not have chosen the experience, they tend to land on their feet and are able to get exciting new employment that puts a new bounce in their step, gets their juices flowing afresh, and leaves them better off in the long run. They find new meaning for work, greater appreciation for the gift of a good job, new satisfaction, challenges, and opportunities to contribute. Yes, it does all come out okay for most people. For those who have transferable skills there is a new niche waiting.

You might be tempted to say "I know it's bad out there, but you can't really know how I feel unless you have had the experience of receiving a lay-off notice." Unless you have lived the experience all the advice is just words. Well, that is a fair statement...but read on.

CHAPTER 2

A Living Testimony

Surviving the Layoff

During the days when jobs were abundant and opportunities plentiful, I had a good job in Denver, Colorado, as Placement Director of the University of Denver when the Executive Director of a major non-profit organization came to a convention that I was chairing. He pulled me aside and asked if I was interested in a job opportunity in Bethlehem. I said "Judea?" and he said "No. Bethlehem, Pennsylvania, a town in the eastern part of the state." We engaged in an on-the-spot interview in the hotel lobby. I literally sat next to a cactus planter and listened as he unfolded an offer I could not refuse. I sold my house, packed up my wife and two kids, and headed east for greener pastures and wide open opportunities in ol' Little Town of Bethlehem.

The job was great. The company did well during the good times and was a great place to work for seven years. However, when a recession struck in the early 1970s and companies cut back on hiring budgets, the non-profit organization was not able to cover the loss until the economy turned around. Although I never really believed they would divest themselves of this valuable service after all the developmental money they had invested, I was wrong! One board meeting in June, they bit the bullet and shut down the entire department. Even if you are forewarned, the impact of the reality can be overwhelming.

That first night I gathered my family around the dinner table and shared the news. (I had already had a private session with my wife.) Immediately, they personalized it in regards to how it would affect their lives.

So here I was with shattered dreams. I had just built our dream home. I had put all my money into the house, I had depleted my savings and gone into debt, I had a wife and four kids and was feeling very vulnerable. I was living from paycheck to paycheck and the skinny severance package and unemployment check was not enough to make ends meet. I was up the corporate creek without a paddle.

I indulged in a "pity party" which lasted a few days and decided to get away to get a new perspective, so I took off for a week of self examination, evaluation, and strategy. When I returned, I turned the corner to enter my office just as I had done for the past seven years and ran smack into a blank wall. While I was gone the carpenters had come and filled in the doorway and painted the wall so it was impossible to see where my office had once been. When my employer sent a message that I was finished, he sent it with an exclamation point!

I remember that our lifestyle changed drastically during those months. We planted a garden and were amazed at how much it supplemented our grocery bill. We absolutely cut out buying clothes, gifts, dinners out, vacations, and all unnecessary expenditures.

It was during this time I began applying all the principles in this book and in a matter of six months I was able to land an excellent job in Boston, Massachusetts.

Although this was a scary experience, I was young, inexpensive, and very mobile. It was a difficult time but not nearly as threatening as when it happened twenty years later. Time passed and when

I was in my mid-50s, at the top of the salary rung for my profession, lightning struck again.

This time it was during the worst recession in thirty years. It came at the worst time possible—we had six kids, with three in college. Two were married and out of the nest, but the college expenses and Southern California's cost of living were high. This time I had absolutely no warning. I went into the boss's office for an annual budget meeting and came out without my job. As the boss continued to talk I scarcely heard his words. The only question that kept going through my mind was "Why?" It couldn't be happening to me again.

I withdrew and could not focus on anything else. The first time it was no surprise; I could mentally prepare myself and my family. This time the complete surprise caught me off guard. I was scared. I replayed the situation over and over again. I felt angry and hurt and my pride was seriously bruised. I even threatened legal action. They couldn't do this and not pay. They did not follow correct procedures. I could get them on wrongful discharge. How would I explain this to my friends? How would I save face? How could I phrase this so I would look innocent—victimized by the situation? How in the world could I find another job in my mid-50s in these tough times?

I went through an emotional roller coaster. I was alternately filled with confidence, energy, and enthusiasm followed by discouragement, lethargy, and withdrawal.

I told myself if anyone could market themselves, I should be able to. After all, I had been dealing with people in job search situations every day for the past thirty years. Surely I would get another dream job. I knew all the tricks and I had a great network and know-how. I had already begun writing this book and it was mostly done. Now I had the necessary time to complete it.

The most pressing consideration was financial, as I constantly had to reevaluate my staying power to hang in there for the job search. Would I run out of resources and be forced to take a job that left me underemployed and miserable? Would employers pass me by for younger and less expensive professionals? Would I lose my house? Would my kids be able to complete college? Would I have to move to some undesirable part of the country?

I was learning again first-hand how a layoff affects every aspect of life: emotions, finances, spirituality, self-worth, self-esteem, socialization, and self-identity.

Somehow deep inside I knew that I had not been abandoned, that I would be delivered from my dilemma and in the fullness of time a golden opportunity would present itself.

This was the time to draw down deep from my spiritual resources, my depth of personal worth, my training, values, psychological adjustment, the core of my being, and learn what I was really made of—and this can be scary in itself. I was afraid I would see little substance to fall back on. In fact, there was much more in reserve than I thought and so I began to draw on that hidden reserve and begin the long struggle up the ladder to another successful career.

Systematically, I began once again to apply the principles in this book. I took no short cuts. I was determined to prove that my age, my circumstances, and my salary requirements would not beat me. I really got a handle on a few principles that I knew but are easy to forget.

Today's career path is a tenuous journey. The rules of yesterday are broken. Job security lies only in yourself. There is no longer any such thing as lifetime employment. Managing my own growth had to be my own responsibility. I needed to take charge of my own career and manage it, set my own goals, and develop a vision for the future that fit me. It was apparent that I needed to diversify my skills in as many ways as possible. I needed to define that vision and make the transition to a new life. I realized I was burned out in my old career, and I needed a new bounce in my step. Twenty-five years of doing the same thing convinced me that it would be a mistake to take a similar job in a different organization. I did define that new career. It looked different than what I had been doing in the past. The new paradigm did stretch me and I found myself in an entirely new kind of work and a totally different lifestyle.

Recognizing Opportunities

People are moving out into new careers that a few years ago they would never have considered if they were attached to the corporate world. The banker becomes the rancher in Montana. The Human Resources Director moves to the mountains and runs a small retail store. An Accountant starts a bed and breakfast in Maine. The possibilities are unlimited and the stereotypes no longer hold water.

Successful job changers use the interruption to stop, contemplate, and plot a new course. Instead of this being a major catastrophe, it can be looked upon as a great adventure leading down a new, unexplored path.

After a four-month job search I began a new chapter in my life-book as Manager of College Relations for a major West Coast bank. It was a significant shift in lifestyles including a long commute but, in other ways, it was an extension of what I had been doing moved over to the other side of the desk. It did put a new bounce into my step and has revitalized my remaining working years.

Now what were those specific steps I took twice to jumpstart my career? The remainder of this book spells out in detail *what to do*!

CHAPTER
3

How Are You Doing On The Job?

Assess Your Standing

Periodically in life it is valuable to assess who you are, where you are going, and how you are going to get there. You should do this at least every five years, ideally at a time when you are not under pressure or threatened in the job. This self-examination all too often takes place near burn-out time, when you are frustrated on the job or just fed up, or as a reaction to outside stimulus.

There are times when it is appropriate to move on to other pastures (not necessarily greener). However, frequently it is better to stay put and let events unfold. This section is divided into two parts. The first part deals with job satisfaction and job burn-out. The second part deals with broad life goals, your ideal job, and so on. Both sections are designed to inspire you as you sit under the juniper tree and assess where you are. As the years go your goals, aspirations, and circumstances may change; when that happens, you have to change and adapt.

Once you determine that a change is inevitable, where do you begin? A job change can be such an overwhelming undertaking that it is difficult to know how to start. So, as with many other tasks, you simply break it down into more manageable components.

Career development is a process that never ends. It continues throughout life. Effective career development requires a specific set of skills, a knowledge of certain concepts, and accurate information, specifically in the five aspects of career development discussed below.

Using the five focus points for career development, you will be able to do the following series of very simple exercises. These will help you to analyze yourself and become a more effective job seeker. Do not draw conclusions from any one exercise, just process the questions. The purpose is for you to identify both positive and negative information about yourself and your working patterns, and to help you determine what your career direction should be. Only an honest, open, and candid self-appraisal will allow you to satisfactorily complete these exercises and generate a realistic personal profile and direction definition. Without these it is unrealistic to assume that you can prepare a resume or conduct an effective interview that truly reflects your capabilities, experience, accomplishments, and potential.

Five Focus Points in Career Development

1. You need an up-to-date understanding of yourself. What are your current interests, values, aptitudes, and abilities.

2. You should have a general understanding of the world of work. There are approximately 40,000 job titles at last count, and you must know how to focus on those that are appealing to you. It is also helpful to have some understanding of the many nonoccupational activities that can add to career satisfaction.

3. You need to be clear on your career and lifestyle expectations. What is it that turns you on? Is it money, status, influence, or the opportunity to make a difference? How will your occupation affect your overall life-style? It is important for you to know your personal payoff system so that you can seek an environment where relevant opportunities exist.

4. Making effective decisions is a concern faced by all of us as we approach mid-career change. There often seems to be a "decision overload." There are decisions about post-college activities, personal relationships, and a number of other concerns. You should know how to make decisions rationally in a series of well-defined steps, and at the same time be responsive to humanistic concerns.

5. You need to learn how to implement the decisions you make. Sometimes people make great decisions, but then take no steps to implement them—either because they lack the skills, or the motivation, or both. There are specific tactics you can use to overcome this difficulty.

Identifying and Evaluating the Satisfaction of Work

This section will help you explore your work satisfaction and burn-out levels. By assessing your happiness where you stand now, you will be better able to determine where you want to go in your career.

The following list describes various kinds of satisfaction that people obtain from their jobs. Study the list and determine the degree of importance you would assign to each, using the scale below. This will help you think about the aspects of work that are most important to you. Once you have given this some thought, you will be better able to quantify your happiness or dissatisfaction with your current position.

Scale - **4 = Very important**
3 = Reasonably important
2 = Not very important
1 = Not important at all in my choice of a career

_____   Independence: Freedom to do your own tasks without significant direction from others; not having to do what others tell me.

_____   Autonomy: Being able to work independently and without interference.

_____   Influence: Being in a position to affect the actions, opinions, thoughts, and tasks of other people.

_____   Control: Being able to manipulate things to your way of thinking.

continued

_____ Bottom Line Decision: Being the person who has to make important decisions that affect the organization.

_____ Final Authority: Being the person who accepts the blame or credit for decisions.

_____ Group Presentations: Making speeches, reports, talk to colleagues.

_____ Teacher: Teaching or training others in how to do the job/task.

_____ Committee Assignments: Working with others to achieve a given goal.

_____ Deadlines: Work best under deadlines; pressure brings out the best in you.

_____ Structure Environment: Enjoy working within parameters where you know at all times what is expected of you.

_____ Job Satisfaction: The bottom line is the personal satisfaction of a job well done.

_____ Challenges: Constantly being pushed by new challenges. Without challenge it is hard for you to get motivated.

_____ Risk Taking: Following a life pattern of taking risks. You seldom take the safe road.

_____ Right School Affiliation: Important to you to attend the right schools and to associate with like people.

_____ Visible Position: Important to be seen by the right people; to be observed by the bosses.

continued

_____ Helping Society: Doing something to contribute to the betterment of the world.

_____ Public Contact: Dealing with the public on a day-to-day basis.

_____ Computer Work: Work at a terminal getting a task done.

_____ Working with Ideas: Best when you can be creating new ideas.

_____ Intelligence: Important for you to use your intellect and be surrounded with other smart people.

_____ Affiliation: Being recognized as a member of a particular organization.

_____ Friendships: Developing close personal relationships with people as a result of working together.

_____ Managing Others: Having a job that requires you to manage other people.

_____ Expert: Being the acknowledged expert on site.

_____ Aesthetics: Being a person who studies and appreciates the beauty of things and ideas.

_____ Security: Keeping your job and pay no matter what.

_____ Awards: Receiving recognition, awards, and plaques for your performance.

_____ Outside Work: Being outside and working in the elements.

_____ Task Changing: Constantly doing something different.

continued

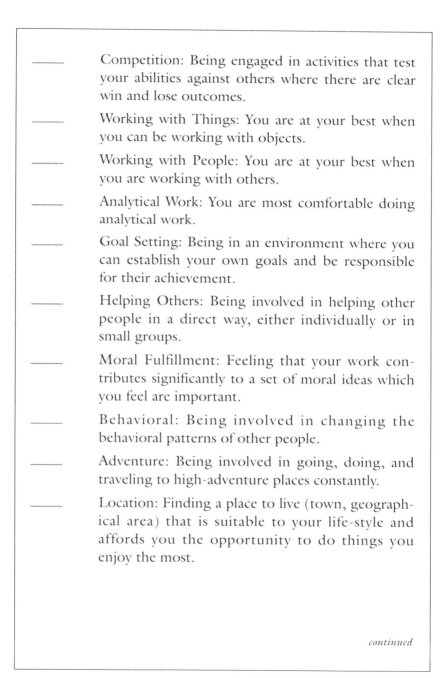

_____ Competition: Being engaged in activities that test your abilities against others where there are clear win and lose outcomes.

_____ Working with Things: You are at your best when you can be working with objects.

_____ Working with People: You are at your best when you are working with others.

_____ Analytical Work: You are most comfortable doing analytical work.

_____ Goal Setting: Being in an environment where you can establish your own goals and be responsible for their achievement.

_____ Helping Others: Being involved in helping other people in a direct way, either individually or in small groups.

_____ Moral Fulfillment: Feeling that your work contributes significantly to a set of moral ideas which you feel are important.

_____ Behavioral: Being involved in changing the behavioral patterns of other people.

_____ Adventure: Being involved in going, doing, and traveling to high-adventure places constantly.

_____ Location: Finding a place to live (town, geographical area) that is suitable to your life-style and affords you the opportunity to do things you enjoy the most.

continued

Notice that there are no right or wrong responses for this exercise. Every individual's priorities are different. However, looking back over your list it should be easy to see which areas take on the greatest significance in your working life. Now you can apply those priorities to your present job, to see how it measures up.

Work Satisfaction Quiz

Scale - 0 = Never
1 = Rarely
2 = Sometimes
3 = Fairly often
4 = Frequently
5 = Very often/Always

_____ Has work become dull?

_____ Do you fantasize or daydream during the day?

_____ Does the job give you the challenges/rewards it did in the past?

_____ Do you dread Monday mornings?

_____ Does depression or melancholy come over you toward the end of weekends/vacations?

_____ Do you experience sickness/headaches that you know are work related?

_____ Do you look for ways to come in late and leave early, or look for chores to do during the day that keep you from your work?

_____ Has your attitude toward working extra hours deteriorated?

_____ Do you feel trapped in your job? Do you feel your job is "the same old thing"?

_____ Does your performance measure up to what you know it can be?

continued

_____   Are you finding it harder to get out of bed in the morning?

_____   Have you lost your concentration, enthusiasm, and will to succeed on the job?

_____   Do you wish you were working somewhere else?

_____   Do you feel you are in the wrong job/career?

_____ Total

Score   **50 or more**   = **You are over the edge— you had better make a change.**

21 - 49   = **You need to take this test in four months to see if there is a change in attitude.**

20 or fewer   = **You and your job are well matched.**

Facts About Stress

Companies pay heavily for stress. Consider the following facts.

- The cost of "executive stress" ranges as high as $20 billion annually in workdays lost, hospitalization, and related costs.

- There are 30 million workdays lost to high blood pressure every year, creating an estimated loss of $2 billion annually.

- On-the-job stress affects the health and productivity of an estimated 60 percent of workers.

- More than 550 million workdays are lost because of stress-related illness.

- Approximately 60–80 percent of all industrial accidents are stress related.

- Stress-related worker's compensation claims have jumped more than 600 percent since 1978. The average on-the-job-stress award exceeds all other occupational disease claims.

Life changes, whether sudden or predictable, situational or developmental, for better or for worse, have an effect on all of us. The effect is termed *stress*, and stressful situations—those environmental conditions or situations that require some sort of adjustment or change on our part—are called *stressors*.

Though you may experience stress in your own unique way—as muscle tension, a short temper, stomach pains, dizziness, tension headaches, fatigue, or any one (or more) of an almost infinite variety of symptoms—physiological changes characteristic of stress are the same for everyone. The involuntary responses that make up the stress syndrome include:

- Increased blood pressure

- Increased heart rate

- Increased rate of respiration (breathing)

- Increased flow of blood to the muscles, and

- Increased metabolism

This set of responses, called *the stress response* or *the fight or flight response*, has been a part of our physiological makeup for perhaps millions of years. For our primitive ancestors, and for us, such a highly developed set of reactions increases the chance of survival. Indeed, because of its utility, it would be incorrect to say that the stress response is necessarily bad or detrimental. Physical and physiological preparedness for fight or flight in dangerous situations is still of critical importance to our welfare and survival.

However, the stress response is elicited in many situations unknown by our ancestors. Such situations, which may be intermittent or developmental, are those in which our bodies are required to work overtime—increasing our blood pressure, heart rate, rate of respiration, and metabolism. When we are not able to react appropriately to stress, which is most of the time, the fight or flight response may ultimately lead to heart attacks, strokes, ulcers, fatigue, kidney disease, and other diseases. It can also lead to psychological problems: insomnia, withdrawal from others, irritation, depression, and extreme or bizarre behaviors and thoughts.

Despite the fact that there is a set of stress responses common to all people, situations stressful to one person may *not* be stressful to another. In general, stress is a function of a person's physical and mental state. You have undoubtedly noticed how both your health and your mood affect how you react to people and events. What (or who) may be stressful to you at one time, may not be so at another. How we feel both physically and mentally profoundly influences our responses to life events.

Whatever the cause is, the symptom is very real and frequently expresses itself in a burn-out attitude. The following exercises will allow you to test your attitudes toward stress on the job. Realize all people suffer varying degrees of stress on any given day or season. If it is ongoing or consistent then you need to do something about it.

Stress Indicators

Five Common Warning Signs of Stress

1. **Inefficiency.** The quality and quantity of your work goes down.

2. **Job Dissatisfaction.** Nothing about your job ever seems right.

3. **Fatigue.** You feel like you're always running on empty.

4. **Sleep Disturbances.** It becomes hard to fall asleep, and you often wake up in the night and think about work.

5. **Escape Activities.** You try to escape from your problems rather than deal with them.

Four Main Causes of Stress

1. **Time Pressures.** The days never seem long enough to get everything done.

2. **Inadequate Feedback on Performance.** You continually worry about how you're doing.

3. **Unrealistic Expectations.** You want to be number one, and you're often unwilling to accept less.

4. **Lack of Goals.** Without a specific direction at work you often waste valuable energy, and sometimes find yourself at a dead end.

Techniques for Controlling Stress

1. **Take a Stress Inventory.** Make a specific list of everything that causes you stress. Discuss your list with someone you trust and respect.

2. **Control Your Time.** Learn how to effectively handle the telephone; how to say "no"; how to set goals; and how to handle drop-in visitors.

3. **Improve Your Self-Talks.** Make that little voice in your head work for you instead of against you.

4. **Reexamine Your Expectations.** Accept the fact that some things about your job can't be changed and concentrate on the things you can change.

5. **Be More Assertive.** Improve your communications with the people at work.

6. **Improve Your Fitness and Diet.** Keep your mind in shape by keeping your body in shape.

7. **Expect and Prepare for Change.** Be flexible. View change as a challenge rather than a threat.

Rule Number 1
Don't sweat the small stuff.

Rule Number 2
When managed well, it's all small stuff.

Symptoms of Burn-out

Lethargy—extreme sleepiness, inactivity, can't get work done on time when in the past it was no trouble

Projects you used to enjoy are no longer enjoyable; drudgery has replaced job excitement

Irritable, edgy, snippy, short tempered

Feeling overwhelmed—too much to do and too little time

Loss of energy, creativity, and new ideas

Defensive and paranoid; making excuses for work not being done

Feeling alone and alienated; no one understands, cares, or takes an interest in what you are doing

Negativity or pessimism, critical spirit, always looking on the negative side of things

Difficulty sleeping; can't get enough sleep; difficult getting out of bed and going to work

Abuse of alcohol or drugs

Difficult to live with at home; moody, angry, mean, unnecessarily lash out at spouse or children

Feel rigid, stubborn, and inflexible

Extreme daydreaming, making excuses to be away from work

Restlessness; inability to relax

Not able to process job performance criticism, job evaluations, suggestions to improve

High absenteeism or tardiness

Clock watching

On edge; small problems that you used to cope with easily are now big sources of irritation

Inability to concentrate or focus

Blame everybody but yourself for mistakes, or blame yourself and feeling guilty because you hate work

Physiological symptoms such as twitches, ulcers, gastrointestinal problems, rashes, indigestion, weight changes, headaches, hives

Extremes in caring; either you stop trying to care, or you care too much

Loss of interest; feeling detached or turned off by everything

Personalizing all comments and criticisms; taking everything personally

Inability to deal with stress

The Five Damaging Stages of Job Burn-out: Where Are You?

Stage One: The Honeymoon

A period of enthusiasm and job satisfaction that nevertheless begins to use up valuable energy reserves

Stage Two: Fuel Shortage

Increasing job dissatisfaction and inefficiency; fatigue coupled with sleep disturbances; escape activities such as smoking, drinking, drugs, shopping sprees

Stage Three: Chronic Symptoms

Debilitating symptoms such as chronic exhaustion, physical illness, acute anger, and depression set in

Stage Four: Crisis

A period of deep pessimism, self-doubt, and obsession with problems. Physical illness grows from discomfort to incapacity. Development of an escape mentality: the flight response.

Stage Five: Hitting the Wall

Career and life are endangered.

Burn-Out Quiz

This quiz is designed to help you assess the burn-out-producing potential of your work environment. Rate the degree
to which the following statements apply to your work setting, using the following scale:

Scale -   1 = **Does not apply at all**
             2 = **Applies very little**
             3 = **Applies somewhat**
             4 = **Applies to a considerable extent**
             5 = **Applies very greatly**

1. Absenteeism and turnover are problems.   1 2 3 4 5
2. Office politics are a way of life.   1 2 3 4 5
3. Employees are afraid to express
    their true feelings.   1 2 3 4 5
4. Organizational change and growth are
    resisted.   1 2 3 4 5
5. Supervisors demand obedience from
    their subordinates.   1 2 3 4 5
6. Productivity focuses on individual achievement
    while teamwork is deemphasized.   1 2 3 4 5
7. There is a lack of company-sponsored
    programs to improve workers' physical
    and emotional well-being.   1 2 3 4 5
8. Work loads are heavy and
    working overtime is expected.   1 2 3 4 5
9. New employees are left on their own
    to learn their jobs and meet fellow workers. 1 2 3 4 5

continued

10. Threats to job security exist.   1 2 3 4 5
11. Supervisors make decisions about jobs
    without involving subordinate employees.   1 2 3 4 5
12. The goals of the company are either
    unstated or unclear.   1 2 3 4 5
13. Regularly scheduled time-outs such as
    coffee breaks are lacking.   1 2 3 4 5
14. Physical/environmental hazards and
    nuisances go unattended and are neglected.   1 2 3 4 5
15. Employees have little autonomy.   1 2 3 4 5
16. Promotion and pay increases depend on who
    you know and on the whims of those in power. 1 2 3 4 5
17. Making profits is more important
    than solving employee work problems.   1 2 3 4 5
18. Advancement/promotions come slowly.   1 2 3 4 5
19. Employees are expected to develop
    new work skills on their own time
    and at their own expense.   1 2 3 4 5
20. Fellow employees appear to be burning out.   1 2 3 4 5

Total _____

(add all circled numbers)

Score 25 - 35   = **Very low burn-out-producing potential**

36 - 50   = **Low burn-out-producing potential**

51 - 70   = **Moderate burn-out-producing potential**

71 - 90   = **High burn-out-producing potential**

90+ or more = **Very high burn-out-producing potential**

When You Have Been Laid Off

Managing Your Perceptions

Professional managers are frequently over-invested in their careers. As one lady stated, "My life was my job, but now I'm finding out how wrong that is." A person's self concept can come from being a money producer. Although this is true of all professional people, it is particularly true of middle-aged, successful males. Respect and prestige are anchored to job roles. If your life is your job then when you lose your job you can feel betrayed by your employer and stressed at home.

When you have been laid off, there are many emotions that immediately overwhelm you: Failure, inferiority, anger, frustration, self-incrimination, pity, self justification, fear, panic, rejection, and many others. You undergo a wilderness sensation—lost feelings, feeling cut away from familiar surroundings. Former associates at work may not know how to cope with your loss so they begin to withdraw from you. After being away from each other for months, they greet you with "You don't have a job yet? How horrible." They may mean it in good spirits but it becomes discouraging. Your confidence gets shaken, your emotions go up and down. After being laid off you begin with great enthusiasm but, sometime along the way, you hit the ropes or run out of gas, energy, direction, and just sit down and molt. This painful time forces self evaluation and makes you reconsider the realities of life. It causes you to step back and re-evaluate what is really important.

It can be a dark time in personal growth, but it also can be useful and productive and force you to understand why you are following the path you are. It can force you to make decisions rather than just go with the flow.

Downsizing affects all walks of life; it reaches beyond the executive suite and into our personal lives. My son-in-law in Boston was called into the President's Office at 3:45 P.M. The president informed Scott and everyone else in the organization that they were terminated effective immediately. No two-week notice, no severance pay, benefits ceased at the same time, even the normal 30-day grace period for benefits was waived because the company had filed for Chapter 11. My son-in-law has a one-week-old baby (my second grandchild), a wife recuperating and not working, an $1,100 house payment due the first of the month, and bill collectors knocking at the door. He has very marketable skills but the job search took time and the financial pressure did build.

It is hard to believe some of the stories of how people were handled when they were presented with a "pink slip." George (a fictitious name) went to work on Friday as he had for the past 17 years. At 10:00 A.M. his boss called him into his office and informed him he was terminated on the spot. Very little explanation was offered. He was assured it was nothing of a criminal nature, or even his job performance (he had recently had a successful job review). It was just one of those things, caused by downsizing. There was a security guard standing there to usher him out of the building immediately. He was handed his final paycheck with sick leave and vacation time rolled in. He was told his personal belongings would be at the front security desk at 2:00 P.M. and that he was to hand in his I.D. and keys, and the locks on his office door would be changed. He was ushered out of the office, down the stairs, and onto the street.

The company had found it necessary to handle his severance this way because it was an aerospace defense facility with highly sensitive data that George had access to. It was concerned that George, if given the usual two week notice, might damage or sabotage the existing programs. Management just couldn't take the chance.

There are cycles of emotions that you may experience when you are laid off. Even if you suspect that it is coming, the impact of the reality can be overwhelming. It is even more severe if you are unsuspecting.

A Positive Search Plan

Just as objectives must be set and an action plan developed prior to beginning any project, a positive search plan will be invaluable to you in terms of timely and meaningful return on your personal investment. The objective that you seek is a new career direction. A well organized and positive plan will make your candidacy unique and specific to your needs and will allow you to overcome your competition. A less than positive plan will result in no opportunity or one that is taken out of a sense of urgency. Your search is a full-time occupation and must be handled in the same professional fashion that you would a full-time position.

You must learn to control your mind and be a positive thinker in order to convince others that you are the most viable candidate for the position. It is possible that your present situation will cause you to react in a very emotional and subjective fashion, thus preventing you from taking the positive steps you would normally follow in dealing with an everyday business or personal problem.

If you keep some basic thoughts in mind, you should be able to cope with the situation:

1. Your experience in business, whether limited or extensive, has given you some degree of exposure to a variety of environ- ments and types of personalities.

2. Your education and/or business training will be considered valuable assets when an employer evaluates your credentials.

3. You have motivation, enthusiasm, and a sense of personal and professional ethics.

4. You have the support of your employer in helping you secure a new direction.

Obviously a major consideration for you will be the timing of your job search. Although you might be eligible for unemploy- ment compensation, this income will not allow you to maintain your present standard of living. (Note: Be certain to immediately check with your local Department of Employment Services office to determine your eligibility.) However, it will afford you the op- portunity to retain a sense of self-confidence and independence. You must be prepared to apply yourself in a conscientious fashion every day, perhaps for an extended period of time. Therefore it is imperative that you pursue a new direction in as positive a fashion as you approached your previous position(s).

There is no reason to feel embarrassed about candidly dis- cussing your situation with relatives, friends, or even a potential employer. The individual who lets pride stand in the way will find that the assistance that would have been given and which may have proven to be of value will not be forthcoming. Do not exhib- it a negative attitude toward or place blame on your employer for your circumstances. It is obvious that sometimes poor supervision may be a contributing factor to a layoff. However, a new employer will view negative remarks about a past or present employer as sour grapes. This kind of attitude will not be regarded favorably in the interview situation. Those prospective employers who do view such complaints favorably may themselves be potential problem bosses. Remember to continue to act in the same professional fashion during your job search as you did when you were em-ployed. Your search will certainly have its ups and downs but don't be discouraged. The downs are temporary and will eventual-ly be replaced by a permanent up.

The next section will deal with preparing yourself for the search if you have been released as a result of organizational downsizing. You will find that you must be candid in identifying your strengths and weaknesses as they relate to your personal and professional ex-perience and skills. Be realistic about yourself and about your ex-pectations.

The chapters that follow will help you prepare for the search, through the process of doing a self-analysis, developing a personal profile, and defining your new direction realistically. First, and most importantly, however, you need to get your finances in shape. Only then can you be prepared to undertake an effective executive job search.

Financial Commitments

Following are those procedures that *must be completed by you* prior to preparing your resume and actively entering the job market.

Family

It is imperative that your immediate family be advised of your total circumstances as soon as possible. Without their understanding, support, and active participation, the home environment will make it practically impossible for you to function on the outside in a rational and productive fashion. A spouse, child, and/or parent should be made to feel a part of the process. After all, they have feelings that will be affected by your situation. Remember, this is a team effort.

Finances—Short, Mid and Long-Term

Review and complete the items listed on the cash flow chart as accurately as possible, with your spouse or family. This exercise will allow you to generate a realistic budget. Without this, it will be difficult to determine what kind of comfortable time frame you have for the job search. In addition, meaningful budgeting will relieve some of the economic pressures that may negate your positive efforts to become employed once again.

Be objective and direct as you review your finances. Don't let egos and social pressures affect your conclusions. Reach mutual decisions on all issues—be cooperative with your spouse in developing a realistic budget.

In considering your budget time frames, these reference periods can be used:

- Short term—three months

- Mid-term—three to six months

- Long-term—six to twelve months

The average search will take six to nine months and if your salary is in six digits it can easily take more than a year of concentrated work to land a new position.

1. Short-Term Action Plan—Finances

    (a) Compare the total due you and due out.

    (b) If the total due you is greater than the total due out, then you are probably* in good shape for the short term.

    (c) If the total due you is equal to or less than the total due out you may have cash flow problems.

*assuming valid cash flow analysis and continued control over fixed and controllable expenses.

If C is the case:

   (i)   Don't rush to sell assets.

   (ii) Don't commit to financing to cover short-term obligations.

  (iii) Don't refinance your home or other large capital assets.

  (iv) Review your controllable expenses and eliminate or reduce accordingly.

   (v) Contact creditors (if possible, in person) and explain the situation. Arrange for moratorium or interest-only payments and stress your credit record. *Document the contact and pay each creditor something each month.*

2. Mid-Term Action Plan—Finances (with your spouse)

  (a) Make a comparison as in number 1 above.

  (b) If cash flow problems exist, continue appropriate activities from number 1. Also do the following:

  (c) See your banker and discuss the feasibility of a plan for:

     (i)   Debt consolidation

    (ii) Applying assets as collateral for a loan

3. Long-Term Action Plan—Finances (with your spouse)

If cash flow problems still exist after implementing plans in number 1 and number 2, consider:

Selling family assets. Use a banker and/or financial consultant for guidance and counseling.

General Guidelines for Cash Flow Control

1. Use your past check registers to identify areas of expenses that can be drastically cut or eliminated.

2. Register with the Division of Employment Security.

3. Stop purchasing anything but the essentials.

4. Begin to defer some bills (e.g., retail, but not utilities).

5. Contact all creditors.

6. Keep documentation of all creditor contracts as a record of your good faith efforts.

7. Negotiate payments on big bills.

8. Be certain to work out payment arrangements for state and federal taxes.

9. Explore the possibility of your spouse and other family members obtaining temporary jobs.

10. Continue to maintain the best basic health and life insurance coverage possible.

11. Investigate low-interest loans against the cash value of your life insurance policy.

Cash Flow

	SHORT-TERM MONTHS 1 2 3	MID-TERM MONTHS 4 5 6	LONG-TERM MONTHS 7 8 9 10 11 12
A. Due You			
1. Severance/Vacation			
2. Unemployment compensation			
3. Savings (cash)			
4. Stocks/bonds (cash value)			
5. Dividends			
6. Interest			
7. Other family income			
TOTAL DUE			
B. Family Saleable Assets			
1. Home			
2. Auto(s)			
3. Vacation home, etc.			

4. Stocks/Bonds
5. Furniture
6. Appliances
7. Leisure vehicles, etc.
8. Art collections
9. Investments
   TOTAL SALEABLE ASSETS

C. Assets as Collateral on Loan

1. Home
2. Automobile(s)
3. Stocks/bonds
4. Cash value - insurance
5. Leisure vehicles/appliances, etc.
6. Vacation home
   TOTAL ASSETS FOR COLLATERAL

D. Fixed Expenses

1. Mortgage
2. Rent
3. Taxes

	SHORT-TERM MONTHS 1 2 3			MID-TERM MONTHS 4 5 6			LONG-TERM MONTHS 7 8 9 10 11 12					
4. Insurance premiums												
5. Regular installment												
6. Other												
TOTAL FIXED EXPENSES												
E. Controllable Expenses												
1. Home operations												
2. Transportation												
3. Food												
4. Clothing												
5. Entertainment												
6. Personal allowance												
7. Cleaning/laundry/housekeeping												
8. Grooming, etc.												
TOTAL CONTROLLABLE												

F. Cash Flow—Short Term   1   2   3

1. Total due you
2. Total due out
        Difference

(see number 1(a) Action Plan Finances)

G. Cash Flow—Mid-Term   4   5   6

1. Total due you
2. Total due out
        Difference

(see number 2 Action Plan Finances)

H. Cash Flow—Long-Term   7   8   9   10   11   12

1. Total due you
2. Total due out
        Difference

(see number 3 Action Plan Finances)

CHAPTER

5

Self-Assessment: Personal Profile Development

The Idea of a Self-Concept

In order for you to know yourself fully, it is important for you to understand all aspects of yourself. The following are what I call the "juniper tree exercises." You find a juniper tree, or any kind of tree, sit down, and figure out the rest of your life! It is worthwhile for you to take the necessary time and thought to work through these exercises. You need to get a firm grasp on your achievements, accomplishments, strengths, and weaknesses, and what jobs met or did not meet these characteristics so that you can articulate these clearly in the job search process. Don't skip over this part of the process or it will be extremely difficult for you to formalize a career direction definition.

Your self-concept is the self you know. To you it represents complete reality. Some of our own images may not be accurate, in that they are not accepted as a part of us by the rest of the world. But that doesn't matter; they are true to us. There are many things we could be, but we don't see these as a part of ourselves, at least not yet.

The self-concept, self-image, or picture you have of yourself is a very important part of reality. It is an interesting subject to explore. Much of our image of ourselves was formed a long time ago and is built or reinforced during adolescence. That self-concept is carried through work life and is particularly important when laid off. Your self concept can be the difference between rolling with the punches or going down for the count.

If the underlying assumption is that professional managers seek successful careers, it is important to understand what success means to you. Success means many different things to many different people. In John Grisham's novel, *The Firm*, success to Mitch McDeere meant being a partner and a millionaire at a young age. Many people today strive for that definition of success. However, my more modest definition of success isn't measured in titles, dollars, or status. Success to me is progressive achievement and realization of worthwhile goals. When goals are realized you keep raising the horizons and there is no limit to how high you can go.

Set worthwhile goals>when realized>establish new ones and start the process over.

This rather simple idea is a lifetime pursuit. Some goals are short term, some may take nearly a lifetime, but never stop striving to be all that you can be.

This definition goes way beyond the work world into avocations, hobbies, and educational pursuits. Circumstances may prevent your work goals being realized, but that does not mean your success goals can't be realized.

He who is not contented
With what he has,
Would not be contended
With what he would
like to have.

Socrates BC 470-399

In my definition, being successfully placed in a job means doing something you enjoy doing and getting someone to pay you for doing it. Getting paid for doing work that you enjoy is a rare find. Success is not defined by money, status, title, prestige, symbols, or even by other people telling you that you are a success. Rather, like most important issues of life, it is internal, it comes from within, it can't be superimposed by other people.

Successfully placed people can be on the lowest rung of the working class or they can be the CEO. I know CEOs who have built major organizations but are not successful. Their assignment is merely a task or a responsibility. It does not bring internal rewards or satisfaction. Yet many janitors are successfully placed.

Success, then, is an attitude, never a destination, seldom a geographical site, and it can be here today in this situation and gone tomorrow in the next situation. It has much to do with your reasons or motives for why you work. It has much to do with your roots—pressures your parents or other members of your family force upon you. I once knew a very successful surgeon in the eyes of the world who had an abundance of money, a lot of prestige, and all the other trappings of success, but was a miserable, unsuccessfully placed person. He couldn't wait to leave the medical profession and do something he could enjoy. This is not an uncommon scenario.

⚘

"The way to success is through perseverance.
Successful people see their failures as stepping stones;
Unsuccessful people see their failures as road blocks."

⚘

Who Are You?

The following exercises will help you come to grips with the real you—your goals, your strengths, your weaknesses, your achievements and accomplishments, and your ideal job.

I am a _____

I am a _____

I am a _____

I am a _____

I am a _____

I am a _____

I am a _____

I am a _____

I am a _____

I am a _____

I am a _____

I am a _____

I am a _____

I am a _____

I am a _____

I am a _____

I am a _____

I am a _____

I am a _____

I am a _____

I am a _____

Broad Life Goals

The following list is by no means complete, but it will give you the opportunity to attach priorities to your goals. Quickly rank in order the items in terms of your own values. It is important to do this exercise quickly without long deliberations. These goals are very broad and may indeed be values. Rank in order the 18 goals from most important to least important.

Number by priority from 1–18.

( ) Wealth —to earn a great deal of money

( ) Service —to contribute to the satisfaction of others

( ) Leadership —to become influential and lead other people

( ) Pleasure —to enjoy life—to be happy and content

( ) Independence —to have freedom of thought and action

( ) Expertise —to become an authority

( ) Acceptance —to be received with approval

( ) Parenthood —to raise a fine family—have heirs

( ) Self-Realization —to optimize personal development

( ) Security —to have a secure and stable position

continued

( ) Prestige   —to become well known and have status

( ) Stability   —to have the ability or strength to withstand change

( ) Duty   —to dedicate to responsibility

( ) Recognition   —to receive acknowledgment or commendation

( ) Affection   —to obtain and share companionship and affection

( ) Professional Accomplishment   —to attain work goals

( ) Intimacy   —to be close to others

( ) Power   —to have control of others

"Whether you think you can or you can't, you're probably right."

Henry Ford

What Are Your Job Goals?

What kind of job do you want?

- ☐ Supervisory
- ☐ Decision making
- ☐ Creative
- ☐ Figure oriented
- ☐ People oriented
- ☐ Physically challenging
- ☐ Mentally stimulating
- ☐ Easy to do
- ☐ Filler with responsibility
- ☐ Mechanical

How much money do you want to make?

- ☐ Enough to make a real effort essential
- ☐ Enough to risk an ulcer
- ☐ Enough to meet bills comfortably
- ☐ Enough on which to get rich
- ☐ Enough for minimum requirements

What fringe benefits do you want?

- ☐ Medical and life insurance
- ☐ Good retirement

continued

☐ Stock options

☐ Part ownership possibilities

☐ Country club and other social benefits

☐ Company car

How about self-satisfaction?

☐ Creative urge satisfaction

☐ Pride in doing something socially useful

☐ A sense of overcoming challenges

☐ A feeling of growth

Where does your future lie?

☐ In building experience for future growth

☐ In accepting more and more responsibility

Your Ideal Job

Position _____

Responsibilities _____

_____

_____

_____

_____

Location _____

_____

Environment _____

_____

_____

_____

Skills Required Which You Now Have _____

_____

_____

_____

Skills Required Which You Do Not Have _____

_____

_____

_____

_____

Salary _____

How This Fits Into Your Broad Life Goals _____

_____

_____

Identifying Strengths and Weaknesses

List your strengths and weaknesses in an objective and honest fashion, then review them with a colleague, friend, or resource person.

STRENGTHS

1. _____
2. _____
3. _____
4. _____
5. _____
6. _____
7. _____
8. _____
9. _____
10. _____
11. _____
12. _____
13. _____

WEAKNESSES

1. _____
2. _____
3. _____
4. _____
5. _____
6. _____
7. _____
8. _____
9. _____
10. _____
11. _____
12. _____
13. _____

14. _____ _____
15. _____ _____
16. _____ _____
17. _____ _____
18. _____ _____
19. _____ _____
20. _____ _____

Maximizing Strengths—Eliminating Weaknesses

List strength maximization and weakness elimination methods according to the strengths and weaknesses outlined previously.

STRENGTHS   How to Maximize

1. _____ _____
2. _____ _____
3. _____ _____
4. _____ _____
5. _____ _____
6. _____ _____

WEAKNESSES   How to Eliminate

1. _____ _____
2. _____ _____
3. _____ _____
4. _____ _____
5. _____ _____
6. _____ _____

7. _____
8. _____
9. _____
10. _____
11. _____
12. _____
13. _____
14. _____
15. _____
16. _____
17. _____
18. _____
19. _____
20. _____

7. _____
8. _____
9. _____
10. _____
11. _____
12. _____
13. _____
14. _____
15. _____
16. _____
17. _____
18. _____
19. _____
20. _____

Sample Strength and Weakness Entries

Strengths	Weaknesses
1. Organizational skills	1. Not self-confident
2. Judgement	2. Cannot make decisions
3. Maturity	3. Unable to verbalize thoughts in an articulate fashion
4. Varied industry experience	4. No supervisory experience
5. Professional appearance	5. Lack of flexibility (i.e., travel, because of family)
6. Sensitivity	
7. Technical audit skills	
8. MBA/CPA	

Sample Strength Maximization/Weakness Elimination

Maximize	Eliminate
1. Apply organizational skills to job search in same fashion as problem or assignment on the job.	1. Identification of and appreciation for strengths should build self-confidence.
2. Utilize good judgment in evaluating job offers and making a realistic decision.	2. Take self-study decision-making course. Generation of self-confidence should develop ability to make realistic decisions.

3. Maturity will give positive sense of direction and create impression of stability and professionalism.

3. Take Dale Carnegie course. Begin to play leadership role in community and/or professional organizations.

4. Varied industry experience opens up job market.

4. Try to generate job situation that will allow for some supervisory experience.

5. Professional appearance will make positive first impression on prospective employer.

5. Set priorities in regard to job and career *vis-a-vis* family. Job market may demand flexibility, (e.g., travel.)

6. Stress sensitivity as a plus *vis-a-vis* potential supervisory capabilities.

7. Technical capabilities should be sold as benefit to prospective employer.

8. Academic and professional credentials will open door to meaningful situations.

Sample Strengths and Weaknesses Profile

I am a mature, well-directed professional with excellent judgmental and organizational skills. My experience is broad. In addition, I have strong technical skills and my academic credentials and business experience are selling features. My appearance is quite professional and combined with my other strengths should make a favorable first impression on a prospective employer.

Although I am somewhat lacking in self-confidence and therefore at times am not decisive enough, I feel that the recognition of the strengths I possess should give me greater confidence in my ability to develop these skills.

I have no supervisory experience, but believe my sensitivity to others and my desire to become an effective manager should allow me to handle some type of entry-level supervisory role.

I must attempt to articulate my thoughts in a more positive fashion, and I realize that this will be a function of my generating more self-confidence.

It is obvious that I must set some priorities relative to my job and family, if I am to achieve a desired level of responsibility within an organization.

Evaluating Your Accomplishments

"Ask yourself, Will it really matter five years from now?"

As part of the analytical process, it is most important to realistically identify and evaluate your accomplishments. The things that you have done well and are proud of will have a major impact on your direction and will serve to give you a sense of self-worth and motivation. Even if others feel that these accomplishments are not meaningful, it is their importance to you that matters.

Whether these achievements are in business, military, family, community, professional, academic, childhood, and/or social situations is irrelevant; the important issue is their impact on your development. *An accomplishment is defined as anything that you liked doing, did well, and derived satisfaction from.*

On page 64, select six of those that are the most significant to you. Briefly describe these in paragraph form. Justify their selection as your most important accomplishments in terms of what *you* did and the results you achieved. Review each of these statements, and then list the accomplishments in order of importance and the reasons why. Be certain to *quantify* the accomplishments listed (where possible).

In continuing the self-analysis process, it is necessary to evaluate your work history as it applies to levels of accomplishment, self-satisfaction, and personal and professional development.

Once this is done, describe in detail the three most satisfying assignments and the reasons why using the worksheet on page 68. Obviously, you should include both the positive and negative (if any) aspects of the position(s).

There are several other areas that you must investigate as you plan your search. Review them and make your comments accordingly on a separate sheet of paper. They are as follows:

1. Are you satisfied with your career progress to date? (yes or no) Please elaborate.

2. How do you spend your nonworking hours? Why do you pursue these activities? Are there other activities that you would like to pursue? What and why? Why aren't you doing so?

3. What are your long-range goals? (personal, professional, and retirement) Why?

4. Outline your earning objectives.

    (a) Next position

    (b) 5 years

    (c) 10 years

    (d) 20 years

5. List the specifics of your education and training.

    (a) formal education

    (b) employment training (on the job)

(c) self-education

(d) business and professional education (non-job)

6. List affiliations with your level of participation in professional, community, and social organizations. Are there others that you would like to pursue? What and why?

7. List all other areas of knowledge and skills not included in any of the other exercises (machines, processes, languages, manual skills, athletics, etc.) How can you utilize them in your search?

Reflecting on the exercises just completed, and as you further implement the analytical process, it is important to evaluate the positive and negative effects that your education and training, interpersonal and intergroup relationships, personal skills, areas of interest, hobbies, community activities, long-term goals (personal, professional, and economic), and career progress to date have had on your situation.

Using the worksheet on page 69, make brief but complete statements relative to these issues. In addition, be certain to list any adverse factors, events, or situations (controlled or uncontrolled) that might have prevented you from achieving your goals. *You must be objective.* Comment on all of the negative factors and ways in which they could have been neutralized.

Upon completion of these exercises, you will be able to identify the kind of career direction that your strengths best prepare you for and that your existing weaknesses will not prevent you from achieving. Obviously, once a direction is identified, you still must concentrate on eliminating your weaknesses; otherwise you may find yourself searching for a new direction much sooner than anticipated or desired.

Page 71 gives an example of the career direction definition process. As you see, there are three columns. The first column should reflect those things you definitely *want* in your next situation; column two, those things you would *accept*, and column three those things you definitely *do not want* and have justification for not wanting.

It is obvious that unless your self-analysis in these exercises is honest and candid, you will be unable to develop a valid career direction definition. A casual approach to, or neglect of, the exercises will severely limit your ability to identify the career direction and objectives that you should be seeking.

Please note the breakdown of your responses. An almost ideal job would be 80 percent "want" and 20 percent "would accept." One will never find the ideal job; however, the opportunity that is accepted must allow for movement in a direction from "accept" to "want" items as opposed to "accept" to "don't want." The majority of jobs would be closer to a fifty-fifty "want/accept" breakdown. However, the potential for movement must be from "accept" to "want" in order for you to seriously consider the situation.

It is possible that timing, your frame of mind, family pressures, and personal finances may cause you to seriously consider a direction that has many more "accepts" than "wants" and perhaps several "don't wants." Do not accept an opportunity that has a valid "don't want" that cannot be resolved. Be realistic in your evaluation of any situation and keep in mind *you do not have anything to turn down until you have something to turn down.* One can always negotiate some of the "don't wants" out of the opportunity once it has been offered; therefore, make every effort to explore any situation that seems reasonable.

Using the guide on page 73, prepare a written summary of the conclusions you have reached relative to your next opportunity. Be certain to comment on all aspects including responsibilities, reporting relationships, work environment, and so on. Do not leave anything unsaid.

My Significant Accomplishments
(in order of importance)

What	Why

1. _____

_____

_____

2. _____

_____

_____

3. _____

_____

_____

4. _____

_____

_____

5. _____

_____

_____

6. _____

_____

_____

My Significant Accomplishments
(description)

Be certain to refer to results, e.g., people, payroll, and cost savings, profit improvements, production, methods, etc.

1. _____

_____

_____

_____

_____

_____

_____

_____

_____

_____

_____

2. _____

_____

_____

_____

_____

_____

_____

_____

_____

3. _____

4. _____

5. _____

6. _____

My Three Most Satisfying Jobs

What   Why

1. _____

_____

_____

_____

_____

_____

_____

2. _____

_____

_____

_____

_____

_____

_____

3. _____

_____

_____

_____

_____

_____

_____

Factors Affecting My Situation
(Positive and negative)

Factors	Comments

1. Education
   and Training

   _____
   _____
   _____
   _____
   _____

2. Interpersonal
   and Intergroup
   Relationships

   _____
   _____
   _____
   _____
   _____

3. Personal Skills,
   Interests,
   and Hobbies

   _____
   _____
   _____
   _____
   _____

4. Community
   Activities

   _____
   _____
   _____

continued

<table>
<tr><td></td><td>_____
_____</td></tr>
<tr><td>5. Long-Term
Goals</td><td>_____
_____
_____
_____
_____</td></tr>
<tr><td>6. Career Progress
to Date</td><td>_____
_____
_____
_____
_____</td></tr>
<tr><td>7. Specific Factors,
Events,
or Situations</td><td>_____
_____
_____
_____
_____</td></tr>
</table>

Next Job Definition—Sample

Want	Would Accept	Don't Want
1. Professional environment	1. Some exposure to other MBAs and/or CPAs.	1. No other professionals
2. Manufacturing or distribution	2. Financial services to round out background	2. —
3. Limited immediate supervisory responsibility with potential for future growth	3. Major supervisory role, initially	3. No opportunity for supervisory experience
4. No travel	4. Limited travel, 10%	4. Travel, 10% +
5. Assistant Controller or Manager of Accounting	5. Controller (small company)	5. Internal audit position
6. Reportability to senior individual	6. Reportability to peer (age, not experience)	6. Reportability to peer (age and experience)

continued

7. Opportunity for technical growth	7. Limited initial opportunity for growth	7. Routine technical responsibilities
8. Position requiring planning and organizational skills	8. Utilization of planning and organizational skills on infrequent basis	8. Mechanical job requiring no planning or organizational skills

Summary—Career Direction Definition
(Complete in detail)

Based upon my completion of these exercises, I feel that my next opportunity should:

_____

_____

_____

_____

_____

_____

_____

_____

_____

_____

_____

_____

_____

_____

_____

_____

_____

_____

_____

_____

_____

Your Resume

Developing Your Most Important Sales Tool

Now that you have defined your direction, it is imperative that you generate the vehicle that will allow you to begin developing employment sources and contacts. Your most important tool during this self-marketing process, in addition to your personal and professional experience, skills, and presentation, is your resume. The primary objectives of your resume are as follows:

1. State the kind of work that you want to do and the skills, accomplishments, and experience that will allow you to do it.

2. Generate interviews through the arousal of reader interest.

3. Serve as a mutual aid during the interview.

Prospective employers may review hundreds of resumes for each opening they have. These resumes usually come in on an unsolicited basis, through personal contacts, newspaper advertisements, employment agencies, and executive search firms.

Because of time constraints and other priorities, prospective employers may screen out most of the resumes that they receive. It might only be the unique resumes that catch their attention. This is not to say that one must use unusual ink or typeface, or colored paper. All it should really take is a professional, well-organized, and unique approach to your resume. Your resume should represent the real you and supply the reader with meaningful information.

Do not throw your resume together in a random fashion or allow some outside organization to prepare it for you. I am occasionally asked if resume preparation businesses are a good idea. In fact, a few people have paid up to $2500 for professional resume services. I can't generalize about all of these services, but I personally believe that if you follow the guidelines put forth in this book you will never need to spend your money in this way. However, you will need to invest time and thought into writing your resume.

1. Keep your resume brief, logical, and no longer than two pages.

2. Build on your strengths and quantifiable accomplishments. Never make assumptions about the reader's ability to interpret impressive titles, adjectives, or buzz words as reflecting professional ability and/or potential on your part. Clearly describe your skills and abilities.

3. Be certain that your resume reflects your strengths, not your weaknesses, and that it is directed toward the opportunity(ies) you identified through thoughtful self-assessment.

4. Your resume need not be so detailed that it tells your whole life story. Leave enough room for imagination and positive prejudgment. This will make the prospective employer want to meet you on a face-to-face basis to learn more about the interesting individual whose general qualifications and accomplishments are reflected in the resume.

5. Emphasize measurable, quantifiable accomplishments (e.g., greater sales, payroll savings, decreased costs, increased reliabil-

ity, efficiency, adherence to schedules, beating budgets and improving profits, etc.).

There are a number of questions that you should be asking yourself as you prepare your resume. These questions can be answered by the information generated through your self-assessment.

1. What do I want to do?

2. Why am I justified in having this objective(s)?

3. What have I done for my present and past employer(s) that I could do for someone else? (accomplishments quantified)

A prospective employer reviewing your resume will want to know the following:

1. What does this individual want to do?

2. Why is the individual justified in having that objective(s)?

3. What has the individual done for someone else that could be done for me? (accomplishments quantified)

Remember that the resume is the vehicle that will carry you to a first interview ahead of your competition. It must present you as a unique and accomplished person with many positive features and potential benefits for a prospective employer.

The first questions in each list are answered by your statement of objective. The objective may be general if your experience is not extensive or if you would rather not limit yourself to a particular position or work environment. On the other hand, if you have certain skills or an extensive amount of job and/or industry experience, it would be prudent to be as specific as possible. Otherwise the prospective employer might misinterpret the general nature of your job objective as being a lack of direction on your part. The objective should be the first item on the resume and should answer the first basic "must" questions.

Any objective, especially one that refers to a specific and/or senior type of assignment and challenging environment, will cause the more experienced resume reader to ask why the individual is justified in wanting to achieve that level of responsibility and be exposed to that kind of environment. Therefore, you might want to include a "qualified by" section to answer the second questions on the lists. One's ability to assume responsibility, utilize experience and education, make a contribution to profitability, and develop professionally can all be justified by a "qualified by" or "summary of qualifications" section similar to those in the sample resumes. The main purpose of this section is to answer the second basic "must" question and to keep the reader motivated and enthusiastic about continuing to review your resume. It is also used to give added credibility to your objective and general credentials.

The third basic "must" questions must be answered in the experience section. The description of your experience should be action oriented and quantified statements of accomplishments. Your accomplishments, though perhaps common to most individuals in similar situations, are presented in a fashion that gives them uniqueness. The accomplishments should be quantified and reflect the bottom lines. In many cases, resumes present responsibilities of the position as items that are routine, mundane, and not results oriented. Describing accomplishments will present your experience as unique, action-oriented activities that reflect a decisive and highly motivated individual. Your experience might not be any different from the next person, but the fact that you are presenting it in a meaningful and unique fashion and format will tune in and turn on the reader while answering the third basic "must" questions. The reader will hopefully finish reviewing the experience section and say, "I must interview this individual because of the uniqueness and relevance of the accomplishments listed." Even though the reader might be quite familiar with the basic responsibilities of a person performing a similar function, he or she will still be very positive about the unique and unusual method in which you have presented yourself. In preparation for writing this section, it would be helpful to refer to the listings of your specific accomplishments. You can then utilize those that are of prime interest, impact, and relevance.

The educational and personal sections of the resume must now be included in the same fashion. Educational data should be brief and direct, outlining academic background, eliminating grades, honor societies, scholarships, and all other activities that may only be meaningful for the individual seeking a first job. *Note:* This kind of data may be discussed during a second or third interview. But in most cases, when you are seeking a second or third job, it will not be relevant to the process of establishing an initial contact.

An organized and brief educational and personal section will be supportive to the other parts of your resume and should give the reader a more positive initial feeling for not only your professional qualifications, but your level of intelligence and stability.

It is usually not necessary to refer to military experience unless it relates to your current objective and is used to point out the administrative, technical, management, or special skills gained while a member of the armed forces. Obviously, be certain to refer to the chronology of military service if the absence of same would leave a large and unexplained time gap in the experience section of the resume.

References should be eliminated from your resume in all cases. When the interview process reaches the point of supplying references you can then attend to it. It is usually not necessary to supply references to generate a first interview. You will find that in some cases, a personal reference can be mentioned in the cover letter that accompanies your resume.

Information regarding your present salary and or future salary requirements should be omitted from the resume. It is best to eliminate any reference to salary until you are at the point where a prospective employer questions it. The only time one should reference present salary and/or future requirements prior to an interview is if this data is requested as part of initial candidate information.

Your resume should reflect your self-profile and career direction definition. It should be unique, hard-hitting, and decisive. It is the first exposure that a prospective employer and/or resource person will have to you, and it must have the high impact and positive uniqueness that will set it aside from any other resume received. A resume should be professionally typed and printed. Keep in mind that first impressions are most important and that you as a professional must strive to make that high impact impression.

A Guide to Preparing Your Resume

General Guidelines

Because there are so many books on the market on how to write a resume, it is not my purpose to go into much detail, but it is important to discuss some of the elements of how to prepare a professional resume. A resume is one of the most important tools needed to implement a successful job campaign.

More than 95 percent of all professionals are introduced by a resume. The purpose of a resume is to obtain a job interview. It will not get you an automatic job offer; however, a good resume can be the key to obtaining an interview.

Your resume should be a brief, informative summary of your abilities, education, and experience as they apply to your career goals. As you begin to prepare your resume, remember that it is not a biography, it is a profile—one which should highlight your most important assets.

The resume reflects who you are. However, its content, format, and length should be geared to the type of job you are seeking. Although resumes should take on the personal characteristics of the writer, these are guidelines that should be applied in presenting your qualifications on paper. Resume format is subject to trends. The resumes in this book include the most up-to-date formatting information available.

The process of preparing a resume really begins long before you sit down to write. First you must identify your career goals and then take a thorough inventory of your abilities, education, and experience. Only then can you draw a clear picture of yourself. The key is to maximize your strengths and minimize your weaknesses, while presenting an accurate picture.

You should also bear in mind that employers receive so many applications daily that your resume may only get someone's full attention for 20 seconds. It is therefore important to utilize carefully the little space you have!

Start by preparing an outline. Next, prepare a draft. Evaluate the draft, edit it, and condense it. There is always time to revise and improve *before* you have your resume printed.

A resume consists of *words,* so it is important to choose them wisely. Avoid excess baggage. Do use strong action verbs, but do not use personal pronouns. Other basic guidelines of resume writing are as follows:

Do

- Use an outline format.

- Make it easy to read. Appearance is important. A five-second glance leaves an impression.

- Use spacing, underlining, bolding, and capitalization for emphasis. Graphically, the resume should be easy to follow and pleasing to the eye.

- Be consistent in content and format.

- List entries in reverse chronological order (most recent position first).

- Avoid time gaps when possible. However, if you do not want to talk about something, you may leave it off the resume.

- Put category headings in order of priority. For example, people with a significant amount of work experience may choose to put the employment section ahead of education.

- Use 8½ x 11 good quality paper. Use a light-colored paper such as off-white, light gray, ivory, or any other soft color.

Do Not

- State responsibilities as opposed to accomplishments.

- State salary information.

- Include a picture with your resume.

- List your references.

- List health status.

- Leave obvious chronological gaps.

- Limit yourself geographically.

- List reasons for leaving previous employers.

- Omit names of present and past employers.

- State all the facts about yourself.

- Be overly modest, provide the reader with the best information about yourself.

- Include any negative connotations, extreme superlatives, repetition, and/or jargon.

Any of these "don'ts" may lead to some negative prejudgment on the part of a prospective employer which could prevent even an initial interview. In addition, they could result in your resume being screened-out with all of the others that reflect the same errors in resume preparation. It is important that your resume sell not only your features but the benefits of having those features within the prospective employer's organization. It is imperative that you stress your strengths and quantifiable accomplishments in a unique and positive fashion.

Formats

There is no one universally accepted format for preparing a resume. In fact, there are various formats that meet individual needs. In this book you will find examples of five different types of resumes: chronological, functional, achievement, composite, and curriculum vitae.

The *chronological* resume is blocked into sections categorized by *source* of skills, (for example education and work experience). Items in each of these blocks are listed in reverse chronological order. This type of resume is appropriate for persons possessing enough employment experience to support their career objective. As your employment history lengthens, you may elect to eliminate some early jobs from the resume, the later positions being more applicable to current career directions.

The *functional* resume is categorized by the skills possessed, spotlighting marketable skills for the employer to review. This format enables one to de-emphasize employment history and allows focus on one's transferable skills (aptitudes or talents that can be applied in a number of settings). This type of resume is particularly appropriate for those who have had one major job, those making career changes, and those who have not had direct experience in the field being pursued.

The *achievement* resume highlights specific achievements that you have accomplished as a function of prior work experience. For persons whose work is quantifiable, this type of resume may be a good fit.

The *composite* resume incorporates and integrates components of the functional, achievement, and/or chronological resume. A composite format may be developed to best suit your needs. For example, if past work experience no longer supports the new job objective, it may be appropriate to de-emphasize the places where you worked and emphasize the transferable skills you hope to use in the new capacity sought.

The *curriculum vitae* or *academic* resume is a resume geared toward educational settings, because teachers, professors, administrators, and other educational staff may need to incorporate academic considerations into the picture presented to a potential employer. Their resumes include credentials/certification, courses qualified to teach, research and publications, academic honors, thesis or dissertation topics, grade point average, professional presentations or lectures, academic associations, language competencies, and other information pertinent to an academic career objective.

Information

The following are some suggestions to help you structure individual categories within your resume. Pay close attention to the information that could be included in each section and select those elements critical for your resume and for the positions you are seeking.

Identification

- Name

- Address (present/permanent)

- Telephone number (home and work or message)

Career Objective

- This is the most important element of your resume. Most studies show that goal-directed behavior is much more likely to produce positive results and obtain the interview. The rest of the resume should support the stated objective. If you have more than one objective, it is recommended that you prepare a separate resume for each career direction.

Education

- Emphasize the positive aspects of your academic career and extracurricular activities. Describe any academic honors or scholarship you have received as well as any positions of leadership you have assumed.

- Degree/major/institution

- Relevant courses (optional)

- Academic performance (GPA, if good)

- Relevant class projects

- Publications

- Professional affiliations/memberships

- Honors/certificates

- Extracurricular activities

Work Experience

- Describe tasks related to the position you are seeking. Emphasize major accomplishments, eliminate minor details.

- Indicate progressive increases in responsibility. Include civic projects, volunteer work, etc. This category includes both paid and unpaid positions.

- Be specific and avoid vague generalities.

- Do not overlook periods of self-employment; include all employment experiences, summer and otherwise, as appropriate.

- When describing current employment, use present tense; when describing past employment, use past tense.

- Include:

    Position title
    Name of employer
    Location
    Dates
    Brief job description (use bullet format)
    Level of responsibility
    Include accomplishments as well as duties

Background Sections

- These sections can include information that would not ordinarily be found under any other category heading. Some examples are:

    Language fluency
    Achievements
    Honors
    Skills
    Computer skills
    Community activities
    Professional affiliations
    Presentations and/or publications
    Related experience

- It is against the law for employers to request information about race, sex, age, marital status, or physical health, and these elements *should not* be included on a resume.

Interests

- It is a good idea to include three or four of your personal interests. This information adds some color to your personality on paper and is often an icebreaker in an interview. Avoid listing such general activities as reading, music, or sports, as most people enjoy these interests. It is much more colorful to say, "Enjoy 19th century American literature, bluegrass and jazz music, and competitive lacrosse."

- The key is to differentiate yourself from every other candidate, and this section is an ideal opportunity to do this.

References

- The phrase, "References Available upon Request" is self-explanatory and need not be included. If desired, a separate sheet listing the names, addresses, telephone numbers, and relationship (to you) of your selected references may be prepared to submit upon request.

Action Words

Describe your experience in terms of what you have accomplished. Use action verbs, adverbs, and adjectives for strengthening your descriptions of your experiences. This approach is much more powerful then merely describing duties or responsibilities.

Accelerated	Edited	Maintained	Reduced
Actively	Effected	Managed	Reinforced
Adapted	Eliminated	Motivated	Reorganized
Administered	Established	Negotiated	Researched
Analyzed	Evaluated	Operated	Responsible
Approved	Expanded	Organized	Revamped
Built	Expedited	Originated	Reviewed
Chaired	Founded	Participated	Revised

Completed   Generated   Performed   Scheduled
Conceived   Guided   Pinpointed   Set-up
Conducted   Implemented   Planned   Solved
Contracted   Improved   Prepared   Streamlined
Controlled   Increased   Presented   Structured
Coordinated   Influenced   Produced   Supervised
Created   Initiated   Proficient   Supported
Delegated   Interpreted   Programmed   Taught
Demonstrated   Launched   Proposed   Trained
Designed   Learned   Proved   Wrote
Developed   Lectured   Provided
Directed   Led   Recommend

Functional Skills

The following list of skills will help you as you prepare the Employment Experience category on your resume. Expand upon the list as needed.

Instructing/teaching   Promotional work
Computing quantitative data   Helping others
Debugging programs   Processing ideas
Helping others personally   Language usage
Organizing people   Record keeping
Public speaking   Treating ailments
Dramatic presentation   Drawing diagrams
Selling products   Making decisions
Meeting the public   Laboratory work
Obtaining information   Correspondence
Coaching for performance   Computer work
Inventing new ideas   Outdoor experience
Coordinating events   Counseling others
Managing other people   Library research
Legal activity   Serving as mentor

Entertainment
Supervising others' work
Analyzing quantitative data
Synthesizing technical data
Media, graphics
Creating with your hands
Organizing data
Planning programs
Training others
Writing
Money transactions
Safety operations
Vocal tasks
Fundraising
Negotiating
Organizing leisure

Collecting information
Interviewing people
Social arrangements
Solving problems
Selling ideas
Electronic data
Confronting others
Managing information
Mechanical work
Design of inventory
Researching in field
Creating displays
Scientific work
Organizing
Investing
Writing instructions

Sample Chronological Resume

KIRSTEN ANDERSEN

45 Sewall Avenue
Los Angeles, California 91234
(213) 555-3412

Objective
A marketing position, preferably in the consumer products industry, utilizing analytical, organizational, and interpersonal skills.

Education
MBA, The Anderson Graduate School of Management
University of California at Los Angeles;
May 1994
Concentration: Finance and Marketing
- Awarded tuition fellowship and teaching assistantship.
- Member, Graduate Management Student Association; elected President, 1991.

B.A., University of Wisconsin, Madison
Major: Sociology, May 1989
- Honor Society.
- Secretary and executive board member of Alpha Epsilon Phi Sorority.

Experience
Financial Control Analyst Trainee
1990–Present
Bradford Trust Company of Los Angeles
- Manage daily demand deposit accounts.
- Interact with custodian bank, insurance companies, and clients.
- Reconcile individual accounts, requiring extensive contact with client base.

Kirsten Andersen
Page 2

Blood Bank Coordinator 1982–1990
Thomas Jefferson University Hospital
- Monitored patient billing and crediting.
- Controlled purchasing and inventory.
- Analyzed department and physician blood utilization.
- Calculated department statistics.

Affiliations   American Marketing Association
Los Angeles Women in Management

Skills   Fluent in Spanish and French.
Familiar with LOTUS 1-2-3, SPSSx and BASIC.

Interests   Have traveled extensively throughout Europe, Central America, and the United States.
Enjoy camping, kayaking, jazz, and gourmet cooking.

Sample Chronological Resume

MARGARET R. PETERS

1111 China Avenue
Claremont, California 91711
(909) 555-8853

CAREER OBJECTIVE

Administrative position in higher education, utilizing my education and experience in communication, supervision, and developmental counseling and programming.

EDUCATION

Ph.D., Northwestern University, Evanston, Illinois
Major: Higher Education Administration: August 1993
G.P.A. 3.9/4.0
Dissertation: *"The Effect of Proactive Programming on Residence Life in the Small College Setting"*

M.Ed., James Madison University, Harrisonburg, Virginia
Major: Counseling; May 1986
G.P.A. 3.7/4.0
Emphasis on college student and young adult development

B.A., University of Virginia, Charlottesville, Virginia
Double Major: Psychology and English; May 1982
Summa Cum Laude

Margaret R. Peters
Page 2

PROFESSIONAL
EXPERIENCE

Dean of Students and Course Instructor
Harrison Preparatory School,
Claremont, California 1987-Present
- Responsible for administration, counseling, and developmental programming at a preparatory school for high-potential learning disabled adolescents.
- Teach two year-long courses: Psychology, and Literature and Creative Writing.
- Serve as liaison to the residential program and general campus administration.
- Administer disciplinary proceedings, including confrontation, parental interaction, and implementation of sanctions.
- Advise the Student Council, student-initiated programs, and college bound seniors.
- Conduct small-group therapy work with students.

Assistant Dean of Students
Schmidt College, Los Angeles, California
1984–1987
- Responsible for overall administration of the residence life program, including housing, placement, and billing.
- Selected, trained, and supervised residence life staff of 7 hall directors and 38 resident assistants.
- Supervised the Health and Counseling Center, Student Government Association, handicapped students, and the commuter and married student population.

Margaret R. Peters
Page 3

- Coordinated the production of the Student Handbook and "Guide to Residence Life."
- Chaired the Publications Committee; served on the Admissions Committee.
- Coordinated the nomination and selection of recipients for several college and national awards.

Counselor
Schmidt College, Los Angeles, California 1982–1984

- Personal counselor for individuals and small groups.
- Coordinated "Faculty/Staff In-Service Seminar Series."
- Conducted Values Clarification groups for women students.
- Worked with students on stress reduction and management.
- Dealt frequently with student issues including bereavement, eating disorders, depression and suicide, self-concept, sex roles, and adjustment difficulties.

Residence Hall Director
Jones College, Harrisonburg, Virginia 1978–1982

- Responsible for total administration and direction of co-ed residence halls; including developmental programming, training and supervision of student staff, personal and group counseling, discipline, being an on-call resource.
- Team-taught course in "Leadership Development" for student staff.

Margaret R. Peters
Page 4

- Responsible for academic advising and counseling for a group of freshman undecided majors.
- Chaired the faculty "Cultural Affairs" committee.
- Created and edited "The Hall Suite Journal," a student development publication.
- Conducted seminars on a variety of topics relating to student development for students and faculty/staff.

ADDITIONAL EXPERIENCE

Coordinator, "Project Amigo," a service project bringing 50 college students to Costa Rica for a 3-week, intensive exposure to the realities of a developing country.
- Served on central planning staff.
- Trained and supervised students in fundraising techniques.
- Team-taught preparatory coursework.
- Mentored and supervised women students in preparation and on-site.
- Led small and large group discussions regarding the experience.
- Supervised work site at village orphanage.

Additional Travel throughout England, Ireland, the Caribbean, and the United States.

PROFESSIONAL PRESENTATIONS

"Creating Effective In-Service Programs for Faculty/Staff"—N.A.S.P.A. National Conference, 1989

"The Grieving Student"—N.A.S.P.A. Regional Conference, 1987

Margaret R. Peters
Page 5

PROFESSIONAL   National Association of Student Personnel
AFFILIATIONS   Administrators (N.A.S.P.A.)
                                  Phi Delta Kappa
                                  Lambda Iota Tau, Literary Honor Society

Sample Chronological Resume

Note: The following two examples illustrate a successful transition
from a chronological to a functional resume.

SUSAN CHARNEY

111 Maple Street, Apt. 21   Home (909) 555-5548
San Bernardino, CA 92345   Work (909) 555-3344

CAREER OBJECTIVE

A managerial position in operations, preferably with line authority
and in an ambulatory care setting.

SUMMARY OF QUALIFICATIONS

Fifteen years of steadily increasing responsibility in health related
industries, including several years in administration, planning, and
analysis of systems and procedures. Have extensive experience in
budget management, with line and staff assignments including
supervision of 12 staff members. Skilled at interacting with all
levels of staff and management.

EDUCATION

University of Denver, Denver, Colorado
Master of Business Administration: Concentration: Strategic Planning; Honors, August 1993

- Developed a regional HSA plan and assessed CON proposals
  in light of its standards. Analyzed regional demographics,
  health care needs, and levels of service.
- Forecasted the 1989 GNP based on a detailed trend analysis of
  Consumer Durable.
- Assembled a guide to housing and transportation for 30
  towns/cities—*The Greater Los Angeles Area*—as a
  recruitment aid for California General Hospital's Department
  of Human Resources.

University of San Francisco, San Francisco, California
Master of Science; Concentration in Physiology and Immunology
Cumulative grade point average: 3.69 (4.0), June 1979

SUSAN CHARNEY
PAGE 2

Arizona State University, Phoenix, Arizona
Bachelor of Arts; Concentration in Zoology
Cumulative grade point average: 3.5 (4.0), June 1977

PROFESSIONAL EXPERIENCE:

Thyroid Unit, Phoenix General Hospital, Phoenix, Arizona
First Assistant Laboratory Technologist 1983–Present

- Assess and resolve both administrative and technical problems.
- Coordinate interdepartmental and external agency activities.
- Consult with physicians and others regarding research problems.
- Develop, execute, and interpret research projects.

Infectious Disease Unit, Los Angeles General Hospital,
Los Angeles, California
Senior Research Technologist, 1979–1983

- Conducted immunological investigations.
- Managed lab operations, including purchasing, bookkeeping, and equipment maintenance.
- Prepared data for publications, including literature searches, writing, and graphics.
- Trained technicians, medical students, and fellows in immunological procedures.

MEMBERSHIPS

Healthcare Public Relations and Marketing Association
Graduate Management Student Association

Sample Functional Resume

SUSAN B. CHARNEY

111 Maple Street, Apt. 21	Home (909) 555-5548
San Bernardino, CA 92345	Work (909) 555-3344

CAREER OBJECTIVE

A managerial position in Health Care Operations, preferably with line authority and in an ambulatory care setting.

PROFESSIONAL EXPERIENCE

Phoenix General Hospital, Phoenix, Arizona
First Assistant Laboratory Technologist, Thyroid Unit,
1983 to Present
Senior Research Technologist, Infectious Disease Unit,
1979 to 1983

SKILLS

Management
- Supervise technical and medical personnel in research and clinical activities.
- Establish operational procedures, including troubleshooting of problems and implementing corrective action.
- Administer research and capital expenditure budgets
- Coordinate a broad spectrum of interdepartmental functions and external agency programs.

Analytical and Research
- Verify and quantify scientific data.
- Assist in the development of computer programs and train personnel in computer use and maintenance.
- Organize quality control mechanisms. Analyze results and implement corrective procedures.
- Develop grant proposals.

SUSAN B. CHARNEY
PAGE 2

Interpersonal and Communication
 - Interview prospective employees.
 - Conduct job performance evaluations, including merit and disciplinary determinations.
 - Instruct and counsel personnel in laboratory and hospital procedures.
 - Prepare data for publication including literature searches, writing, and graphics.

EDUCATION

University of Denver, Denver, Colorado
Master of Business Administration; Concentration: Strategic Planning
Honors, August 1993

 - Developed a regional HSA plan and assessed CON proposals in light of its standards. Analyzed regional demographics, health care needs and levels of service.
 - Forecasted the 1989 GNP based on a detailed trend analysis of Consumer Durables.
 - Assembled a guide to housing and transportation for 30 towns/cities—*The Greater Los Angeles Area*—as a recruitment aid for California General Hospital's Department of Human Resources.

University of San Francisco, San Francisco, California, June 1981
Master of Science; Concentration: Physiology and Immunology; G.P.A. 3.69 (4.0)

Arizona State University, Phoenix, Arizona, June 1979
Bachelor of Arts; Concentration; Zoology; G.P.A. 3.5 (4.0)

MEMBERSHIPS

Healthcare Public Relations and Marketing Association
Graduate Management Student Association

Sample Achievement Resume

LINDA L. MONTGOMERY

11562 River Lane   Res. (213) 555-7399
Mission Valley, California 94154   Bus. (714) 555-3358

A results-oriented professional with over 20 years of increasing levels of responsibility within the manufacturing field.

General Operations Manager—Managed and controlled a multi-plant $150MM oil-tool manufacturing facility with over 800 employees and $14MM annual operating budget.

Plant Manager—Introduced and directed the implementation of a Group Technology Concept for the manufacturing process.

Division Director of Purchasing—Organized and implemented divisional purchasing, material control, and traffic organization of over $40MM in annually purchased goods.

Director of Purchasing—Organized, sourced, and coordinated the procurement of over $30MM of materials and services from international and domestic sources for seven manufacturing facilities.

SIGNIFICANT ACCOMPLISHMENTS

General Operations Manager

- Effectively organized and administered a new "Start Up" pilot manufacturing facility, including leasing, plant layout, equipment acquisition, and complete staffing.
- Established and managed a program that increased productivity by 30%.
- Introduced and implemented Cycle Count Technique, resulting in inventory accuracy improvement from 67% to 93%.
- Improved customer service level from 75% to 92% on-time delivery.
- Designed and introduced a Quality Improvement Program that resulted in a 7% - 10% reduction in scrap and rework.

Linda L. Montgomery
Page 2

- Restructured the traditional three-shift organization to an Area Supervisory Configuration with improved production efficiency through span of control.
- Successfully resisted a union organizing attempt through a well-planned and executed employee communication strategy.
- Conceived, developed, and implemented an in-house Production Operation Training Program as a source for skilled labor in a tight labor market.

Division Director of Purchasing
- Restructured and implemented a new Divisionalized Function to cope with growing demands for critical materials and services during a period of rising prices.
- Served on task force to negotiate a contract for the construction of a Drilling Bit Plant in the Soviet Union.
- Sourced and negotiated contracts for purchase of capital equipment and critical materials for new start-up plants in Singapore and Aberdeen, Scotland.

Director of Purchasing
- Developed a new organizational Group Purchasing Procedure for seven manufacturing plants.
- Standardized purchasing practices, lowering materials costs and improving quality of service.
- Evaluated plant purchasing personnel and made necessary improvements.

Purchasing Manager
- Introduced and implemented the Value Analysis Concept to the purchasing function.
- Established a standard cost accounting system for purchasing materials and services.

EMPLOYMENT HISTORY

Anderson Packers Division—Anderson Oil Tools, Inc.

General Operations Manager, Colton, CA	Nov. 85–Present
Plant Manager, Fort Worth, TX	Oct. 82–Nov. 85
Division Director of Purchasing, Fort Worth, TX	Jan. 80–Oct. 82

Linda L. Montgomery
Page 3

Pressure Tool Group of Pressure Industries, Inc.
Director of Purchasing, Franklin Park, IL   Nov. 77–Jan. 80

Market Tool Company—Div. of Pressure Industries, Inc.
Purchasing Manager, Fort Worth, TX   Jan. 68–Nov. 77

EDUCATION

Various management seminars sponsored by AMA,
Harvard University, and Wharton College

Ph.D in Economics
The Claremont Graduate School, Claremont, CA   May 1992

Advanced Management Seminar, Pressure Industries
Certified Purchasing Manager   1987

M.B.A. in Economics
Lamar University, Beaumont, TX   1973

B.A. in Political Science
Pomona College, Claremont, CA   June 1967

Sample Achievement Resume

JOHN CLARK

69 Elisabeth Street
Pomona, California 91767
Phone: (909) 555-1122

PROFESSIONAL OBJECTIVE

A challenging managerial or analytical position emphasizing strategic and organizational development in a large, progressive firm.

PROFESSIONAL HISTORY

1990–Present   **Special Service Unit Manager**
General Telephone Company
Alhambra, California

Accomplishments

Led five-person task force to improve service efficiency and productivity on priority commercial accounts with estimated annual revenue of $5.3 million.

Increased efficiency 25% in six months. Productivity increased 35%, producing annual savings of $800,000.

Developed and implemented many structural and operational changes that vastly improved organizational cohesion, communication, and process flow.

Counseled and assisted the administration of resource allocation and labor relations in a dynamic union setting of 60 employees.

John Clark
Page 2

1987–1990   **Research Assistant**
                 Executive Office of Human Services
                 State of California

Accomplishments

Analyzed effectiveness of California's current employment and job training programs, which serve over 300,000 recipients and are budgeted at $350 million annually.

Outlined proposal to integrate training, job referral, financial assistance, and MIS functions across five agencies, which resulted in formal proposal to combine two departments along those goals; estimated annual savings are $15-20 million.

Evaluated legislation creating a new department of Health and Human Services, focusing on operational and policy impacts that will affect approximately 800,000 citizens with a projected 1982 cost of nearly $1.7 billion of the state.

Participated in the development of two-phase proposal to improve delivery, access, and accountability of the state's health and social services while reducing operating costs by 20% in the first year.

Conducted 17-state survey of health-cost regulation mechanisms, which led to Administration plans to better coordinate its currently fragmented system of rate setting, DON, CON, and oversight.

John Clark
Page 3

1983–1987   **Assistant Policy Analyst**
                   Executive Office of Communities
                   and Development
                   State of California

Accomplishments

Was primary state liaison with cities and towns in broad area of state-imposed costs (Chapter 766, health costs mandated programs) and assessed all regulatory actions for fiscal and administrative impact.

Analyzed role of property tax in California's state-local fiscal relations and generated preliminary state estimate of the effects of Proposition 2 1/2.

Examined fiscal and managerial capacity of state to assume new service responsibilities ($500–$600 million in FY 1982) and advocated increased use of local aid reimbursements ($220 million) and sales tax revenues ($275 million).

Helped formulate and organize series of workshops for local officials designed to improve their management of resources and revenue.

Assisted in the assessment of CARD program applications ($100 million in 1984) and generated data supporting the adoption of the Tax Increment Financing proposal, both programs that encourage local support of community development.

EDUCATION

1993   MBA; The Wharton School,
                   University of Pennsylvania,
                   Philadelphia, Pennsylvania
                   Concentration: General Management/
                   Management Policy

John Clark
Page 4

1986   B.A.; Pomona College,
                            Claremont, California
                            Concentration: Political Science/
                            Policy Analysis

PUBLICATIONS

*"A Plan To Reorganize California's Human Services for the
1980's"*
(Executive Office of Human Resources, 1985)

"The 1984 Cherry Sheet Review"
(Executive Office of Communities and Development, 1985)

PERSONAL

Hobbies include antiques, jazz and deep-sea fishing.

Sample Composite Resume

MARTHA WHITE

966 Moore Street
Colton, California 95511
(909) 555-1234

Objective   A senior management position.

Summary of   Sixteen years of production experience
Experience   involved in all activities concerned with
                         engineering management. Competent to
                         plan and manage broad scope of activities
                         from concept through production. Leader-
                         ship abilities proven by record of profession-
                         al activities and rapid advancement. Sixteen
                         years of production experience. Three years
                         of experience on the operating committee
                         including the development of the current
                         strategic business plan. Completion of
                         EMBA degree has served to sharpen
                         general management skills.

Management   - Participated on executive planning
                            committee.
                         - Prepared staff reports on general
                            business conditions, price trends, lead
                            time and strategy to insure product
                            availability.
                         - Coordinated department programs to
                            satisfy changing needs of sales and
                            manufacturing.
                         - Created and directed new total materials
                            program.
                         - Responsible for Purchasing, Inventory
                            Control, Warehousing, Traffic, and
                            Shipping Departments.

Martha White
Page 2

- Supervised a staff of ten. Established job description. Launched interdepart-ment training program for job mobility. Designed reporting procedures to monitor functional activities.
- Wrote departmental policy and procedure manuals.
- Revamped in-house work order procedure for spare parts program. Only product class to hit quota.
- Initiated open order status reports to management.

Purchasing

- Ten years of management experience in all aspects of purchasing.
- Designed and implemented total procurement program for three-hand stock from $110,000 to $320,400.
- Established cost savings programs which netted $124,000.
- Reduced stock and finished goods inventory $114,000 at Wolverine through effective buying.
- Interacted with vendors to reduce severe cash-flow problems and assure continued receipt of materials.

Areas of Knowledge

Production Purchasing
R&D and MR.O. Purchasing
    Standard/Custom/Large
    Sub Miniature:
        Electronic Components
        Mechanical Components
Purchasing Contracts
Vendor Evaluations
Cost Analysis
Negotiations
Inventory Control

Martha White
Page 3

Computer

- Implemented fully interactive Job Shop Floor control system using a Digital VAC 11/730.
- Assisted in recommendation of action after analyzing Wolverine's operations and conducted a market survey of available computers and software.

Education

Master of Arts, Government; May 1993
University of California,
Santa Barbara, California

Bachelor of Arts, Business; 1982
University of Massachusetts, Amherst

Professional Memberships

APICS, North Shore Chapter

Employment Chronology

1985–1988	Wolverine Corporation, Methuen, MA
1984–1985	Andover Medical, Lowell, MA
1983–1984	Audivox Division, U.S. Surgical, Newton, MA
1979–1983	Medical Oxygen Service Division, Burlington, MA

Personal Interests

Own, train and show Rottweilers at A.K.C. licensed events.
Hold a provisional A.K.C. tracking judgeship.

Outline for Academic Resume/Curriculum Vitae

SCOTT D. SHERMAN

205 Nautilus Drive   Home: (619) 555-4567
San Diego, California 90000   Bus: (619) 555-4321

CAREER OBJECTIVE

College or university teaching position in the field of...

Elementary or Secondary teaching position...

Position in educational administration...

EDUCATION

- List degrees held, and universities where degree was taken.
- Include dates of graduation, and GPA if good.
- Include majors, minors, emphasis. Thesis topics, special research, and dissertation title may also be included.
- Note any additional graduate study taken.
- List credentials held (community college, elementary/ secondary teaching or administration, etc.)

SUMMARY OF PROFESSIONAL EXPERIENCE
(optional - also see functional resume)

A functional breakdown by which administrators, researchers, teachers, and other educators may indicate particular areas of competence.

ADMINISTRATION
COUNSELING
TEACHING
PROGRAM DEVELOPMENT
RESEARCH
CURRICULUM DEVELOPMENT
MANAGEMENT AND SUPERVISION
BUDGET AND FISCAL EXPERIENCE

Scott D. Sherman
Page 2

EMPLOYMENT HISTORY

- Indicate major periods of employment within the field of education.
- Employment may be separated into categories, such as:
  Administration
  College Teaching
  Elementary (or) Secondary Teaching
  Research
  Counseling
  Tutoring
  Etc. (as appropriate for your background)
- List in reverse chronological order.
- Include position title, educational institution, dates employed, major responsibilities.

RELATED EXPERIENCE

- Indicate experience not directly in the field of education, emphasizing transferable skills/functions.

COURSES QUALIFIED TO TEACH

- Appropriate for college/university teaching positions.
- Indicate not only courses you have already taught, but those you are capable of or qualified to teach.
- Specific courses may be named, and/or general areas listed.

REPRESENTATIVE LECTURES AND PRESENTATION

- List topics, locations, and dates.

PUBLICATIONS

- List any publications/published research in field.

PROFESSIONAL ASSOCIATIONS

- List academic/administrative professional organizations of which you are a member.
- Do not list teacher unions.

Scott D. Sherman
Page 3

- Indicate any committee membership or professional activity in which you have been involved.

LANGUAGE COMPETENCIES
- Indicate written, verbal, and/or reading fluency.

COMPUTER SKILLS
- Indicate software and hardware with which you are familiar.

COMMUNITY ACTIVITIES
- If applicable, indicate involvements in community activities.

HONORS/AWARDS
- If applicable, indicate any formal professional recognition you may have received.

RESEARCH
- Indicate research in process and areas of interest for future work.

RELATED SKILLS
- Indicate any related skills (e.g., music for elementary school teacher) which may be of interest to potential employers.

PERSONAL INTERESTS
- Interesting personal activities or interests can enhance the overall picture (e.g., travel, hobbies, etc.).

CHAPTER 7

Cover Letters

Making Contacts by Mail

In order to successfully penetrate your job market, it is necessary to reach those target executives who have the authority to hire you. An interview with such a person that results in an offer should be your primary objective.

The contact process outlined in this section, if properly implemented, will lead to target interviews. Although much of your networking will be verbal, written communication will play a vital role in generating positive results. These letters serve many varied, but equally meaningful purposes.

1. To advise others of your situation and gain visibility.

2. To generate interviews.

3. To develop active contact and resource persons.

4. To respond to advertisements.

5. To follow-up after successful interviews and indicate positive interest and influence the interviewer.

6. To reach others for guidance, referrals, and so on.

7. To negotiate certain aspects of the employment package.

8. To accept, decline, or delay response to an offer.

9. To transmit your resume to agency and search organizations.

10. To follow-up after prospective employer turn-down (e.g., to maintain contact).

There are basic rules of letter writing that you should follow as you prepare correspondence *tailored to each specific situation.* Several rules follow:

1. Create reader interest quickly by immediate reference to the situation, relevant accomplishments, mutual interests, relationships, or contacts.

2. Be certain that your objectives are clearly stated.

3. Tell the reader how you can be of benefit in relation to the company's particular needs (sell your features and benefits).

4. Keep the letter brief. Be quite specific.

5. Be yourself. Use language that you would use if you were talking to the reader.

6. Reference only the positive. Negatives are potential deselectors.

7. Always direct the letter to a specific person. Be certain of correct spelling and title.

8. Ask for a response or action, indicate you will follow-up with a telephone call.

9. Send the original, not a copy, unless situation dictates otherwise.

10. Use good bond stationary with matching envelope.

11. Arrange mailings for mid-week receipt (Tuesday through Thursday are better days for reader attention).

12. Do not exaggerate. Erroneous information can come back to haunt you.

The cover letter and resume are necessary tools in the successful implementation of a creative job search. Cover letters are, in essence, introductory sales letters to potential employers, and they *always* accompany resumes. Your task in finding a job is to differentiate yourself from every other candidate. A good cover letter can do this by motivating the potential employer to read your attached resume and subsequently invite you to interview for the position you are seeking.

Because employers receive hundreds of resumes a day and can only interview a small number of candidates, the cover letter becomes the first step in the screening process. Only a few carefully worded letters stand a chance of getting through an employer's screening maze. A well-written cover letter increases your chances of getting an interview.

Recruitment Today sites a recent study on the value of cover letters. Cover letters are more than just a formality to recruiters, according to a survey conducted by The Transition Team, an outplacement firm based in Troy, Michigan.

Of the survey respondents, 60 percent are CEOs, vice-presidents, or personnel directors at a Fortune 500 corporation. All of these professionals are looking for potential hires who have done their homework concerning their prospective employer. Survey results indicate:

- 96% can tell the difference between a form cover letter and an original

- 95% think cover letters are important

- 94% are impressed when a candidate personalizes a cover letter

- 85% are offended when their name is misspelled in a cover letter

- 77% are offended when their gender is mistaken

- 70% read cover letters thoroughly

- 12% respond favorably to applicants who set a specific day and time to check back

- 3% believe that resumes sent without a cover letter will result in an interview with their company

With the arrival of imaging and character recognition, organizations are scanning resumes into databases for computerized job matching, skill inventory recognition, and executive matching. It is important to remember only the resume is scanned into the system, not the cover letter. Make sure all your pertinent information is on the resume, since it is likely that the decision to interview will be based on the resume rather than the cover letter.

The design of an effective cover letter includes the following formula:

Provocation + Job Objective + Qualifications + Achievements + Interests + Motivation + Personality + Aggressive Close = RESULTS

A good cover letter introduces you to an employer and explains why you are one of the best candidates applying for a job with the organization. To a degree, the cover letter expands upon the resume, but it also gives you the opportunity to add personal flavor to your approach. In making your letter reflect your personality, always keep in mind the audience and industry to whom you are writing. A catchy first sentence, for example, might be appropriate for a marketing position, but it will not be well received in banking. If you can, show your letter to someone in the appropriate industry to get an educated opinion of its effectiveness.

Ten Basic Rules for Effective Cover Letters

1. *Type* each letter or use a computerized cover letter service so that each letter looks individually typed.

2. Letters should be typed in proper business format on 8½" x 11" bond paper that matches your resume.

3. Address each employer by name and title. No one likes to receive or respond to a "Dear Sir" letter—it's too impersonal. Professionals suggest that letters be addressed to presidents of companies so that the correspondence will receive immediate attention.

4. The cover letter is the first example the employer sees of your writing skills and of the way you present yourself. Double check for grammatical and typographical errors.

5. Keep your letter short to ensure holding the reader's interest. Three to five paragraphs is sufficient.

6. Open your letter with a strong, attention-getting sentence.

7. The body of your letter should include facts about your past experience in addition to stressing your accomplishments.

8. In your letter, appeal to the self-interest of the person to whom you are writing. Propose a mutually beneficial association with that employer.

9. Include challenging thoughts to inspire the reader to want to find out more in a personal interview.

10. Be aggressive in the closing paragraph and state some kind of plan of action (e.g., I will call you in two weeks to set up an interview).

Keep a record of all your correspondence and the stage of each application. Below are explanations and examples of ten different types of cover letters you may need to write at some time during your job search.

1. Letter of application.

2. Letter of inquiry/direct mail letter.

3. Letter of appreciation/thank you.

4. Letter of inquiry regarding application status.

5. Letter of acknowledgment.

6. Letter giving or seeking additional information.

7. Letter declining offer.

8. Letter of acceptance.

9. Alumni networking letter.

10. Marketing letter.

The *letter of application* (Samples (a)–(d)), also called the letter of transmittal, is used when you know of a specific job opening and you apply directly for it with your resume enclosed. This cover letter should serve as an introduction and can be used to highlight certain qualifications or objectives for the job which may not be immediately apparent in the resume. The cover letter can also be used to stress transferable skills and experience particularly relevant to the job for which you are applying.

The *letter of inquiry/direct mail letter* (Samples 2(a)–(c)) is used when you have defined the specific kind of job you want, when you have thoroughly researched companies or institutions for whom you want to work, and when you can articulate how your background and experience would fit into the organization selected. This type of campaigning is helpful when you want to investigate a large number of prospective job openings. Thoughtful preliminary research is a prerequisite for obtaining positive responses to your inquiries.

A *letter of appreciation or a thank-you letter* (Samples 3(a)–(b)) to the interviewer after an interview emphasizes the sustained interest you have in obtaining the position. Your personal note will keep your name fresh in the employer's mind. Since this basic courtesy is often overlooked, your response will make you stand out from other job applicants.

The *letter of inquiry regarding application status* (Samples 4(a)–(b)) may be used before or after your first interview to find out the status of your application. If you do not hear from the company for a long period of time, it is perfectly acceptable to inquire when the company expects to make a final decision. A long period of time can be defined as three or four weeks or as one week after the date set by the interviewer to be in touch with you.

The *letter of acknowledgment* (Sample 5) is a courtesy that informs the prospective employer that you received the offer and are in the process of deciding. Include in the letter a date by which you plan to make your final decision. In some cases, however, the employer may have informed you when the decision must be made.

Letters seeking or giving additional information (Sample 6) are important if you have any questions or concerns. Do not hesitate to let the prospective employer know. Asking for additional information will help you make a more informed decision. Be specific and clear.

Letters accepting or declining offers (Samples 7–8) let the prospective employer know your final decision. Remember that the employer's staffing plan will hang on your decision. If you accept, plans can proceed for your reporting for work and for your first assignment; if you decline, other candidates must be sought. Do not accept an offer unless you are certain it is what you want. To accept an offer and decline later reflects badly on your university as well as you personally and professionally.

The *alumni networking letter* (Sample 9(a)) and informational interviews are invaluable, and a great way to tap into an existing networking resource. Approaching someone for informational purposes (e.g., to find out more about an industry or position), can often result in actual job leads or references to other influential people. Do not ask such contacts for a job; if your contact has no openings he/she may not want to talk to you. But few people will deny you the opportunity to discuss themselves and their field. Follow up on every lead.

The *marketing letter* (Sample 9(b)) is difficult to write and does not work for everyone. It is a combination cover letter and resume and is usually 2 or 3 pages long. It should be focused on achievements and accomplishments. Stay away from philosophical presentations of your views of business or industry.

Sample 1(a): Letter of Application

1440 Grand Avenue
West Covina, CA 91347
(818) 555-3880
Current Date

Mark Watson
Vice-President of Marketing
American Express
Marketing Research Department
American Express Plaza
New York, NY 10004

Dear Mr. Watson:

Please accept the enclosed resume as an application for the marketing position advertised in the October 1 Los Angeles Times.

I will receive my MBA in marketing from The Claremont Graduate School in May. In addition to my strong educational background, I have had previous work experience in both management and marketing at Polaroid Corporation as a summer intern. This combination of talents, coupled with my demonstrated interpersonal and leadership capabilities, will prove to be a profitable asset to American Express.

The enclosed resume only highlights my qualifications. Therefore, I hope to have the opportunity to elaborate on the contributions I can bring to this position in a personal interview. I will be visiting New York the week of November 29, and would like to set up an appointment with you for that week. I will contact you in the next two weeks to find out which day of that week would be most convenient for a meeting.

Sincerely,

Diane Wok

Enclosure

Sample 1(b): Letter of Application

1302 Commonwealth Avenue
Alhambra, CA 91771
(213) 555-3445
Current Date

Ms. Laura Schumack
Manager, Human Resources
Scovill Manufacturing Company
Management Employee BE 7/80
131 Fremont Street
Hartford, CT 01127

Dear Ms. Schumack:

Your advertisement in the *Wall Street Journal* for a position in operations management greatly interests me as I will complete the Master of Business Administration degree in May. I am presently pursuing a career in manufacturing.

With a good management education and a strong engineering background, I am able to make a profitable contribution to Scovill Manufacturing. As you review my qualifications, please consider that I have
- operations and supervisory experience,
- a proven ability to work effectively with people at all levels of an organization,
- project and contract evaluation experience,
- a demonstrated capability for analytical problem solving.

The enclosed resume briefly details this background and my desire to employ it in manufacturing.

I would like to further discuss with you career opportunities with Scovill Manufacturing. I look forward to speaking with you next week and hope we can arrange an interview at that time.

Sincerely,

Ralph Muncie

Enclosure

Sample 1(c): Letter of Application

3411 Fruit Street
La Verne, CA 91750
(909) 555-3999
Current Date

Mr. Floyd Warrenton
Plumas Unified School District
P.O. Box 295
Plumas, CA 95123

Dear Mr. Warrenton:

This letter of application is in response to the vacancy announcement published recently for a Secondary Teacher of English at Greenville Junior-Senior High School in the Plumas Unified School District.

Attached you will find my California Standard Application form which highlights my teaching experience in both private and public schools in the Southern California Area. You will note that I was hired as a full-time English teacher at the Pasadena Junior High School after having served two semesters there as an intern. This should verify my demonstrated teaching, interpersonal, and leadership capabilities.

My California State Credential was obtained through The Claremont Graduate School in the spring of 1991 and my placement file is being forwarded to you today.

I am certain I could bring some fresh ideas to the English classroom at Greenville Junior-Senior High. I will take the liberty of calling you next week in the hope of arranging a personal interview for this position.

Respectfully submitted,

John M. Barns

Enclosure

Sample 1(d): Letter of Application

3811 Mountain Avenue
Pasadena, CA 92731
(818) 555-8798
Current Date

Mr. Edwin K. Beauchamp
Dean, Personnel Services
Long Beach City College
5709 East Carson Street
Long Beach, CA 90808

Dear Mr. Beauchamp:

Your advertisement in the *Players' Journal* for an Acting Instructor-Director to teach acting classes at Long Beach City College greatly interests me, as I will complete my Master's Degree in Fine Arts and Theater in May 1994.

Enclosed is my resume, which only highlights my qualifications. You will note that my experience includes lead parts in many major productions. Having been involved in theater since the age of 7, I have a well rounded background in theater arts. During the past three years I have been directing plays at the Little Theatre of Claremont, which has starred many students from The Claremont Colleges and local high schools. I am certain that my talents, coupled with years of experience interacting with artists and audiences, would be a great asset to Long Beach City College. My application for a California Credential is being processed at the present time through UCLA.

I would like the opportunity to elaborate on the contributions I can bring to the Long Beach City College Theatre Arts Department through a personal interview. I will telephone your office on Monday, April 8, in the hope that we can arrange a convenient time.

Sincerely,

James C. Carter
Enclosure

Sample 2(a): Letter of Inquiry/Direct Mail Letter

1641 Indian Hill Boulevard
Claremont, CA 91711
(909) 555-9973
Current Date

Paul J. Briggs
President
High Techtronix Corporation
250 Moneyhungry Avenue
Chicago, IL 31112

Dear Mr. Briggs:

In May I will complete the Master of Business Economics degree at the University of California at Berkeley. I am seeking a challenging career opportunity in corporate finance with a high technology firm such as yours.

With a strong quantitative and analytical academic background in investment analysis, capital budgeting, and corporate financial reporting, I possess the financial tools necessary to make an immediate and significant contribution to your finance department. My most recent accomplishments in the private sector demonstrate initiative, a capability for analytical problem solving, and an ability to work effectively with individuals at all organizational levels.

I am certain that your organization could benefit from the input of a highly motivated, proven individual, and would therefore like the opportunity to discuss with you the contributions I can make at High Techtronix. I will call your office next week to arrange an appointment at your convenience. I look forward to our meeting.

Very truly yours,

John Shawin

Enclosure

Sample 2(b): Letter of Inquiry/Direct Mail Letter

1121 South Atlantic Boulevard
Flagstaff, AZ 85223
(602) 555-3385
Current Date

Chip Davis
Vice President
Abraham & Strauss
420 Fulton Street
Fullerton, CA 91111

Dear Mr. Davis:

I would like to propose the addition to your staff of a multi-dimensional manager. Whether employed full-time or as a consultant, I can improve efficiency, cut costs, increase profits. As the enclosed resume indicates, I have managed artists, musicians, and filmmakers. In addition, I have a broad marketing background and have worked on both the agency and client level.

In my capacity as the marketing and administrative manager for a service-business conglomerate, I have achieved the following:

- Increased profits an average of 20 percent when given day-to-day management responsibilities for one company.
- Prepared the business plan and loan proposal to obtain the largest line of credit in the organization's history.
- Divested two unprofitable subsidiaries from the parent organization.

If your company is ready for a proven manager who can contribute to your organization's continued growth, I would like to meet with you.

I will arrive in Fullerton for interviews on April 10 and will call you before that date to schedule an appointment.

Sincerely,

April Applegate
Enclosure

Sample 2(c): Letter of Inquiry/Direct Mail Letter

735 Park Drive
Azusa, CA 91727
(818) 555-3552
Current Date

Stephen W. Hobbs
Corporate College Relations
Data General Corporation
4400 Central Avenue
Rancho Cucamonga, CA 91846

Dear Mr. Hobbs:

In May, I will receive a Master of Information Systems degree with a concentration in management from Massachusetts Institute of Technology. I am interested in a position as a systems analyst in the management of information systems field, emphasizing system structures, design, and implementation.

For the past two years, I have worked for Wang Laboratories as a programmer/analyst for the Finance/Administration and Marketing MIS Departments. In addition, I was employed as a computerized-drafting design programmer for General Electric.

The enclosed resume summarizes my education, professional work experience, and general background. I would be pleased to visit Data General for an interview at a time convenient to you. I will contact your office next week to inquire about your selection process and set an appointment. I look forward to talking with you.

Sincerely,

Huey Larkin

Enclosure

Sample 3(a): Appreciation/Thank You Letter

417 Greenwood Avenue
Indianapolis, IN 47124
(317) 555-3221
Current Date

Phyllis Green
Senior Account Executive
Young & Rubicam
1442 Avenue of the Americas
New York, NY 10001

Dear Mrs. Green:

Thank you for inviting me to Young & Rubicam last Friday, November 11. The visit was most informative and I now have a clear understanding of the junior account executive position. I was impressed with your office and our meeting confirmed my interest in Young & Rubicam.

Please express my appreciation to Bob Stevenson and Jim Perkins for helping to make my interview experience a positive one.

If I can provide you with any additional information to help you reach your decision on my application, please feel free to contact me. I am excited about the possibility of a career with Young & Rubicam, and look forward to hearing from you soon.

Sincerely,

Dawn Bigler

Sample 3(b): Appreciation/Thank You Letter

527 Harvard Street
San Bernardino, CA 91999
(619) 555-7783
Current Date

Ruby Keeler
Personnel Manager
Swanee River Razor Company
5457 Hollywood Boulevard
Los Angeles, CA 90028

Dear Ms. Keeler:

Thank you for inviting me to visit your company on December 8 to discuss a possible future for me with Swanee. The executive training program which you outlined sounds like an exciting one and would give me the opportunity to demonstrate my initiative as well as my interpersonal skills.

It was evident from our discussion that the type of individual who achieves success at Swanee is one who has an entrepreneurial bent as well as one who learns quickly and can assume increased responsibilities. I am confident that I possess all of these characteristics. While at Stanford University, I ran my own small business selling to both wholesale and retail markets. During my work for Starr Enterprises, I advanced rapidly from stock work to sales and then to night manager.

I have included a copy of my marketing research project as we discussed. If additional information is needed to reach a positive decision on my application, please feel free to call me. I look forward to hearing from you in the near future. Thank you again.

Sincerely,

Al Jolson, Jr.

Enclosure

Sample 4(a): Letter of Inquiry of Application Status

49 Freemont Lane
Oakland, CA 94233
(415) 555-3985
Current Date

Harold Murphy, Manager
Personnel Department
Cal-Express
Ontario International Airport
Ontario, CA 91237

Dear Mr. Murphy:

I am writing in the hope of determining the status of my application for a Customer Service Representative position with Cal-Express.

For your information, I met with Kevin Berry on October 13 about opportunities with your airline. He requested that I forward my resume, transcript, and application to your attention, which I did on October 29, 1993.

I would appreciate knowing whether I am still under consideration for this position, as I must make decisions about other job offers by the end of the week. The customer service representative position with Cal-Express is definitely my first choice and I would appreciate your response as soon as possible.

Thank you for your quick attention to this matter. I look forward to hearing from you in the near future.

Sincerely,

Julie Muncie

Sample 4(b): Letter of Inquiry of Application Status

14-B Walnut Street
Ontario, CA 91236
(909) 555-8836
Current Date

John Smith
Director of Professional Recruitment
Aetna Business Forms, Inc.
2008 Lincoln Street
Philadelphia, PA 19115

Dear Mr. Smith:

In November 1993, I submitted my resume and letter of application to you for the opening of your sales management department.

I accepted your invitation to visit your home office on November 19. At that time I met with Mrs. Betty Simpson and Mr. Theodore Dently of the marketing and sales department.

I would like to reconfirm my interest in the position and at the same time ask that you advise me of the status of my application.

Thank you for your attention to this matter.

Sincerely,

Linda Smith

Sample 5: Letter of Acknowledgment

899 Towne Avenue
Pomona, CA 91723
(909) 555-0993
Current Date

William Davis, Manager
Digital Equipment Corporation
150 Coulter Drive
Concord, CA 92345

Dear Mr. Davis:

   This letter is to confirm yesterday's telephone conversation and your offer of employment as Manager of Financial Analysis and Systems beginning November 15, at an annual salary of $86,500.

   I am excited about this opportunity; however, I am considering other job offers at the present time. I will make my final decision by May 15. I hope this does not create any problems.

   Thank you again for your consideration. I will contact you within the next few weeks. Feel free to call me if you have any questions.

Sincerely,

Sue Johnson

Sample 6: Letter Giving Additional Information

56 Norwood Terrace
San Dimas, CA 91769
(909) 555-3657
Current Date

Guido Baskerville
Personnel Manager
ABC Investigative Services
450 Golden Gate Avenue
San Francisco, CA 94101

Dear Mr. Baskerville:

   I hope that by now you have received my resume, transcript, and confirmation of my addresses, as you requested. I have discovered that the Registrar's Office made a slight error on my transcript by omitting my Fall 1990 grade point average of 3.675. It should have been printed above the course listing, as with the previous two semesters shown. The registrar will be sending an official updated transcript with the correction within the next two weeks.

Sincerely,

Laureen Houndsman

Sample 7: Letter Declining Offer

123 Smith Street
Chino, CA 91926
(909) 555-8935
Current Date

N.P. Joseph
College Recruitment Coordinator
Northrup Aircraft Corporation
Burbank, CA 92704

Dear Mr. Joseph:

   Thank you for your letter of May 25, 1993, offering me the position of production control specialist.

   After careful consideration, I have decided to accept an offer with another firm.

   I enjoyed talking with your representative during my plant visit. Thank you for the many courtesies extended to me.

Sincerely,

Neil Jones

Sample 8: Letter Accepting Offer

219 Brookline Avenue
Snowline, CA 91726
(619) 555-0398
Current Date

Katherine Champa
Director
Xerox Corporation
243 Berkeley Street
Berkeley, CA 94273

Dear Ms. Champa:

I am pleased to accept your offer of a position as marketing staff assistant. I will begin work, as agreed, on September 1, at a starting salary of $73,000 per year. I will report to work that morning at 8:00 a.m. in your office.

I appreciate the opportunity to join your staff, and look forward to working with you.

Sincerely,

Jane Appel

Sample 9(a): Alumni Networking Letter

550 Mountain Boulevard
El Cajon, CA 91775
(619) 555-3221
Current Date

Kathy Crosby
Software Manager
ACS Consultants
44 Montgomery Street, Suite 500
San Francisco, CA 94104

Dear Ms. Crosby:

This May I will become your colleague in the ranks of Claremont Graduate School alumni. With graduation nearing, I have two goals: to use my MBA in finance to obtain a position in financial management or analysis and to relocate to San Francisco.

I am writing to you for some firsthand information on what San Francisco is like. I've done some research so I can quote the city's vital statistics, but what none of the reference books talk about is what it's like to live and work there. What is the economic climate? Is there room for another CGS alumnus? Information and advice is what I need most, and maybe you can help me overcome the handicap of a long distance job search.

I will be in the Bay Area the first two weeks of January. I am using this time to set up interviews and talk to people in an effort to get feedback on my search for employment. Since you have already accomplished what I am attempting to do, your input will probably be the most valuable I will receive. I would appreciate any information and advice you can offer. I will contact you by phone next week to arrange an appointment at your convenience.

Thank you for your time and effort.

Sincerely,

Fran Caplan
Enclosure

Sample 9(b): Marketing Letter

1616 Main Street
Los Angeles, CA 90000
(213) 555-8888
Current Date

Ms. Carolyn C. Hire
President
Fantastic Corporation
9999 N. Watson Avenue
Los Angeles, CA 90007

Dear Ms. Hire:

Today, more than ever before, there is a strong need for professionals that are capable of bringing costs under control in such a way that improves productivity and bottom line performance without negatively impacting teamwork, morale and self-motivation.

As Chief Financial Officer of Upslops, Inc., a subsidiary of Very Big Corporation, a $1.6 billion diversified world leader in the manufacture and distribution of computer products, I was responsible for the financial affairs of a $20 million division producing micro chips for the electronic products industry. In this capacity I was able to realize a substantial cost reduction program resulting in 25% in our primary line. I also reduced inventories by over 60% in less than one year, a reduction of over $2 million.

The task was achieved by an ability to cut through difficult problems and reduce them to simple common denominators. My contemporaries consider me to have exceptional abilities to deal with the numbers but also with issues and people within the organization.

Upslops is currently planning a move out of the country due to high labor costs and stiff competition from foreign markets. I have decided to seek another position to challenge my skills and abilities.

Some of my other achievements are:

Developed a long-range business plan at Upslops mapping future business efforts on both short and long term strategies.

Realized savings of over $50 thousand per year installing a new MRP II System.

In human relations, I brought together a circle quality team that built a Value and Lifestyle (VALS) program that addressed long-term employee problems.

Was the lead person on a small merger effort of a small electronic supplier that amounted to a $5 million acquisition.

As CFO, increased net income by 118% during the first year on the job. During the next three years, overall net income was up by almost 150%. This resulted in savings of $2.9 million.

Instituted cost reduction programs which resulted in savings of more than $250 thousand for the past three years; among these were increased machine shop capability and computerized automatic testing capability.

As controller, developed bid rates and reports for use on government contracts preventing loss and lack of control on other major government contracts.

Previous to my current position, I worked for fifteen (15) years at a General Electric electronics manufacturing firm. I began in their training program after my MBA degree and progressed through a series of promotions including Controller and within five years, Director of Finance.

I graduated from the Columbia University School of Management with a concentration in Finance. My undergraduate degree was in History from Pomona College. I am married and will relocate for the suitable position.

I am certain that your organization could benefit from the input of a highly motivated, proven professional and therefore would like the opportunity to discuss with you the contributions I can make to Fantastic Corporation. Please contact me in confidence at my home. If I have not heard from you in 2 to 3 weeks I will contact you again.

Sincerely,

Johnny B. Good

CHAPTER 8

Marketing Yourself

Plan for Success

Getting a job is easy. Arriving at a career is much harder. Achieving a second professional career after age 50 is an amazing accomplishment. There is a great temptation to just continue what you have always done regardless. When forced to change, it affords you the opportunity to assess your goals, dreams, five-year plan, and market realities. Most people would not choose to interrupt their life with a break or unwanted layoff, but many people have profited from the experience and ended up with a bigger, better job that often includes a raise, an opportunity to work out of the house, a generous car allowance, and full line of credit cards. It has been my experience that good things happen to good people even though there is frequently a dark valley you must get through before you come out on the other side. A great attribute of the human species is our adaptability.

The reality is that getting a job is a sales game. But this is often a difficult concept for people to accept. Many say, "I am not a salesperson. I hate to talk about myself or my accomplishments. I know I can do the job. I just don't want to go through the interview process. Can't they see what I can do from reading my resume? Why can't someone just hire me without an interview?" Well it just doesn't work that way. Interviews and multiple interviews are the gate you must pass through before you can fill out a W-2.

So you are selling the most important product in your life— YOU! You may be one of those who has difficulty talking about yourself. If so, that is your growing edge that you must struggle to overcome. Your success in the market may be dependent upon your ability to master this skill.

If you think of marketing yourself in the same way you would market a product, many of the same concepts apply. You need to do market research (self-evaluation), advertising (getting your resume and yourself out before prospective employers), pricing (salary and fringe benefits), market penetration (resume distribution strategies), market segment (knowing who, where, when, and how to contact prospective employers), market follow-up customer satisfaction (feedback and status reports on your application), and competition studies (knowing what other applicants are offering.) The analogy goes on and on. I point these out to illustrate that you really are marketing a product—the most important product you know.

You should use all the tools and resources available to you. In today's tight labor market it is shortsighted to rely on just a few job search methods. You just never know from where that ideal opportunity is going to come. Any reasonable contact should be used, and to ignore a lead based upon hearsay or preconceived notions could prove to negate your efforts. Remember that you have nothing to turn down until you have something to turn down. If a source can be of direct assistance to you or can serve to generate another contact, be certain to utilize it! The end will justify the means as long as the latter involves an ethical and professional process. As your search continues, you will learn more about the sources available to you and can then begin to key in on those that will prove to be most productive for your particular needs. In addition, it is imperative that you make the most prudent use of your time.

Employment Sources

The following are varieties of job search resources and marketing tools.

Networking

Eighty percent (80%) of all jobs obtained today are found through networking. People who know people. Passing the word that in the right situation you might consider a change. Letting the word out through your contacts and in some cases passing out your resume. The goal is for your contacts to hand carry your resume or allow their names to be used with prospective employers. The following is a partial list of networking resources.

1. Friends
2. Relatives
3. Salespeople
4. Stockbrokers
5. Past employers
6. Accountants
7. Lawyers
8. Bankers
9. Teachers
10. School alumni
11. Dentists and doctors
12. Clergy
13. Insurance agents
14. Politicians
15. Fund raisers
16. Individuals who recently changed jobs
17. Small business owners
18. Industry associates
19. Community organization officers

Much has been said about networking. Probably the easiest way to describe the concept is that you contact friends and business associates who can introduce you to their friends and business associates in an ever expanding circle of contacts. The concept is easy in thought, but difficult to follow through. Begin by compiling a list of 20, 50, 75 or 100 names and sort them into priorities in ranking order. Begin at the top of the list and try to set up short meetings, just 15 to 20 minutes, at their offices. Stay away from luncheons and meetings after work. Your goal is two-fold: (1) Have them get to know you and your expertise; and (2) hope for them to be willing to give you a couple of referrals. Ideally, they would pick up the phone and contact their associates on your behalf or allow you to use their names in contacting these people.

Make sure that they understand you are not asking them for a job, but rather for information or suggestions. Don't put them in an awkward position by speaking of a specific job, but rather ask for advice. Say, *"Under the right circumstances I might be making a career change and I would like just a few minutes of your time to receive the benefit of your insights, observations, and contacts in the electronic industry."*

I have found that people love to talk and give advice. They love to talk about their field, industry, and particularly, their own career path. Be direct. Say, *"Let me assure you that I am not going to ask you for a job. I am looking for information at this time."* Suggest 15 minutes as being plenty of time for you to benefit from their information and knowledge.

Be prepared for a variety of responses from, "Come on in" or, "Maybe I could answer a few questions over the phone," to "No, I am too busy." Remember this call is just to get an audience, not to ask your questions. Be appreciative, courteous, and available for their schedule. Normally, it works better if you meet in person rather than over the phone. But, be prepared to ask questions over the phone if that is the offer they extend.

Once you receive a referral, call them and say something like, "I am calling at the suggestion of John Brown who speaks very highly of you in the field of finance. I am looking for an objective viewpoint from professionals in finance about future finance careers in the '90s. I would like advice about opportunities you may be aware of with other organizations. I don't want to bother you regarding specific jobs in your firm, but just thought you might be aware of other happenings in the field. Could you share 15 minutes with me next week?" Or you might say, "Before I plunge too deep into this job search process I would appreciate a professional perspective of my resume and whether you believe I am stating my accomplishments effectively."

Keep a small notebook or a series of file cards with names, titles, addresses, phone numbers, dates, introduced by, comments, follow-up, and so on in your pocket. Be alert for new names and jot them down. Sources of names not only come from newspapers, directories, and other individuals, but also from old address books, gift lists, social calendars, and the like.

Contact each person by phone, and be frank and candid with your contacts. These personal contacts can be meaningful, because any referral by them to another contact and/or prospective employers represents a personal endorsement and a definite advantage for you. Do not let your ego prevent you from contacting anyone for assistance. You will see that the networking process really pays off!

Help Wanted Advertisements

The *Wall Street Journal*, especially the Tuesday and Wednesday issues; the Financial and Week in Review sections of the New York *Sunday Times*; the Sunday edition of the *Los Angeles Times*; other large metropolitan and local newspapers; and related professional and industry trade publications all carry excellent position listings. Don't be afraid to respond to a blind ad especially if you are not in a position where confidentiality is necessary. In the case of open ads (employer and or contact identified), don't be turned off by the company, location, or position/title in question. If the situation seems reasonably interesting, make certain that you respond utilizing your resume and an appropriate typed cover letter. Keep the letter short and use examples of accomplishments that demonstrate your ability to handle the stated requirements. Obviously, your letter should be one that you are comfortable with.

Whenever possible, address your response to a person rather than just an office. Call the company to get the name and title of the person who would receive applications for that position. It is not good practice to answer an ad immediately, but more realistic to wait several days before doing so. In this way, your resume arrives at the prospective employer's or contact's office along with a smaller number of responses as opposed to the large number that usually come in the first few days. The chances are good that in this case your resume might receive a little more individual attention. Most blind box ads are open for two weeks, so that you do have time to respond in a leisurely but still responsive fashion. A prospective employer or contact will normally not be impressed with the fact that you've answered a Sunday ad on that Sunday. It is also prudent to respond to "open" ads that are 30 to 60 days old. Many companies sometimes take months to fill a position and it is possible that your candidacy will still be considered. To that end, check the local library for back copies of newspapers.

Any application instructions stated in the ad should be followed explicitly, especially relative to present salary and requirements. If you are answering an ad that is of real interest, but your background is not a fit, do not send a resume. Instead, use your cover letter to highlight reasons why you could be a fit for that position. Any response to an advertisement should be typed individually and signed by you. Do not give the prospective employer the impression that you are involved in a mass help wanted advertisement response campaign and are using standard preprinted letters. Appeal to the recipient's personal and/or corporate ego by responding directly in original form. Don't be discouraged if you don't receive an acknowledgment of your response to a blind ad or even an open ad. Many prospective employers or contacts don't follow-up on no-interest candidates.

Situation Wanted Ads

It might be helpful to place an ad in the Financial Section of the *Los Angeles Times*, the *Wall Street Journal*, and/or trade and industry journals outlining your general qualifications and asking interested parties to reply to a box number. You are now running a blind ad for yourself and therefore, retaining a certain degree of confidentiality.

Personal Friends, Associates, and Acquaintances

As you begin your search, take the time to sit down and list all of those individuals and their professional and/or business affiliations who might be able to help you. Try to identify those who are "target executives" and have the authority to hire you. Be certain to include others who are active in the industry and/or the type of position in which you are interested. No one should be overlooked, as any seemingly insignificant contact may develop into a meaningful one.

Direct Mail

Another effective job search strategy is a direct mail campaign. This approach only works if you have a broad statistical number of resumes mailed. However, it should be understood that direct mail has a low yield. It's perfectly normal to receive one or two leads for every one hundred letters or resumes you mail. That is the expected response rate, so you are not being realistic or fair with yourself if you consider it an unacceptable return. The normal return is 2 percent. If you get two solid interviews out of one hundred resumes mailed, you are right on target. One of the keys to success in direct mail is your mailing list and its currency.

Recruiting Employer's Report

One of the most authoritative surveys in the recruitment field is made by the Employment Management Association, a national organization of employment and personnel executives. Here are some recent findings from their membership.

1. What recruiting source generated the most candidates for your firm?

newspaper advertising	39%	contingency agencies	8%
employee referrals	15%	job fairs	7%
in-house search	10%	trade publications	5%
campus recruiting	9%	search firms	3%
		other	4%

2. How long does it normally take to fill a vacancy?

four weeks	18%	eight weeks	25%
six weeks	34%	twelve weeks	17%

3. Approximately how many resumes do you receive each week (from all sources)?

1–25	12%	151–250	13%
26–50	17%	251–500	13%
51–100	20%	501 plus	7%
101–150	18%		

4. How many candidates do you interview for each hire (ratio of candidates to hires)?

3	19%	8	13%
4	31%	10	11%
6	16%	15	3%

continued

5. What usually happens when job candidates write directly to the company president?

Forwarded to human resources department
  for response   92%
addressee responds   2%
addressee forwards
  to line management   5%
addressee discards   1%

6. How often does your company create a vacancy for an applicant even though there is no authorized vacancy?

seldom	50%	usually	2%
sometimes	35%	never	12%

7. How do you handle write-ins from individuals?

acknowledge all of them   81%
respond only if interested   14%
discard without responding   2%
file without responding   3%

Source: Employment Management Association

Some startling facts surfaced out of this study. *First, 92 percent of the CEO's forward a resume to the human resource department.* If the human resource person gets a letter with a notation in the corner from the president, you better believe they will act upon it. Second, 81 percent of organizations still try to acknowledge write-ins from individuals. This is probably more true of smaller organizations than larger ones. And third, 37 percent of the time an opportunity is created for an applicant even when one doesn't exist.

There is considerable confusion regarding employment agencies, executive search firms, headhunters, retained search, outplacement, and career specialists. The following should clarify the distinctiveness of each type of organization.

Employment Agencies

Employment agencies normally limit their efforts to representing individuals who are actively looking for new employment opportunities within the local area. When an organization contacts an agency to fill a specific job opening, the agency usually reviews its files for applications from people with appropriate backgrounds and may place ads in local newspapers to attract additional applicants.

Employment agencies are paid by the individual applicant or employer only when a placement is made. They make the majority of their placements in the lower salary ranges. Their payment is a fee based on the employees's starting salary. Fees may be regulated by the state, and frequently follow the pattern of a 5 percent minimum plus 1 percent for each $1,000 of the annual salary of the individual employed, up to a maximum of 20 to 30 percent. Some states also permit an advance fee or charge to the individual who lists himself with an employment agency.

Obviously, there are good and bad agencies. The latter may shuffle resumes and refer candidates to situations where there is no mutual interest. On the other hand, good agencies are professionally and ethically managed. These organizations will give sincere, professional guidance and counsel. It is most realistic that you gain access to a limited number of agencies specializing in your area of expertise and interest. This base can be broadened as your search continues. You will find that with a positive presentation and a well-conceived resume based upon a valid self-assessment and career direction definition, employment agencies will probably be more responsive to your candidacy.

When you establish contact with an agency, be certain that the counselor assigned to you is an individual you will be able to trust and respect, and with whom you can have a good rapport. This type of person will do a very conscientious job and will be certain that you are matched only with situations that may be mutually beneficial. You will then not be referred randomly but as a part of a very well thought out process. In any event, discuss your objectives regarding the position with your agency counselor before you agree to an interview. Also, ask that the counselor not send your resume to anyone without first advising you. Do not in any case sign a contract with an employment agency that requires you to pay a fee for any of the agency's service. You should be quite certain of your obligations and indicate that you will only consider situations that are employer fee paid. Remember, agencies work on a contingency basis and the amount of effort put forth on your behalf will depend on the return the agency expects on its investment. However, if you approach a reputable agency in a professional, positive and decisive fashion, the agency will probably work hard for you. Using newspapers, telephone books, and or references, choose three agencies that handle openings in your area of interest, contact them by phone, and proceed accordingly.

Employment agencies are the same thing as headhunters. They work for the individual and collect a fee based on a percentage of the agreed salary almost always paid by the employer. Usually they deal with lower salary ranges. Staff turnover is extremely high since they are paid on commission. Many people are just waiting for the right job to come across their desk, and then they are gone. Because staff turnover is so high it is often difficult to develop long-term relationships. Unfortunately, most executives find little help through employment agencies.

Executive Search

Executive search firms do not work for the individual but rather for the employer. The fee is prearranged and is either on contingency or retained basis. When a key CEO moves from A to B in the same industry it is usually through the help of a search organization. It is unethical for a company to approach a prospect directly so they do it through a third party, an executive search firm. If the employer does not have a person in mind, then it is the job of the search organization to locate the appropriate person. This translates into identifying, screening, and presenting three perfectly qualified people to fill the position. A major consideration is the chemistry between the organization and the applicant.

Most search organizations attempt to deal with key executives. Korn Ferry, the largest search firm only deals with searches of $85,000 and up with the majority of their business in the $300,000 to million dollar range!

Search firms do not want your resume or want you to stop in their office. But it's my experience that they won't throw away your resume if you send it to them. In fact, many will put it into a firm-wide data base to be searched on behalf of future assignments. They also do not like to deal with unemployed people. They would rather have you happily employed. They then place the golden phone call and say, "I have a client who may be interested in a person with your experience. Do you know anybody interested in making a job change?" Expect that 95, 97, or even 100 percent of the search firms you contact won't have anything for you at any given time.

The search consultant who uses the contingent fee approach must fill the position before his fee is paid by the client, and this can change the entire rationale of the assignment. There is a strong tendency for some recruiters who conduct contingency searches to spend as little time as possible on a search, to refer as many candidates as possible, or to compromise standards by referring mediocre or marginal candidates to the client.

The economics of the contingency fee arrangement force the recruiter to accept far too many assignments and to favor filling positions quickly or not at all. Since fees are not collected unless and until a candidate is hired by the client, a major commitment of time in the interest of quality results is not economically feasible. Hence, the contingency approach encourages recruiters to become brokers in executives. This method cannot usually be relied upon to obtain well-qualified talent for important client positions, and the top professional search consultants do not use it. There are, however, many recruiters who work on a contingency basis, and some have done remarkably well. Some contingency recruiters conduct personal interviews and reference checks and differ from their retainer counterparts only in mechanics of payment.

Retained search is one in which a client retains a recruiter to identify and appraise executives well-qualified to fill a specific management position. An initial down payment is followed by progress payments, and the full fee may have been paid before the position is actually filled.

Outplacement

Outplacement organizations have sprung up over the past 10 to 15 years to provide a service to employers who are laying off employees. These firms are paid by the employer and work with two kinds of employees—key executives and lower level groups of employees. Executives receive counseling, use of a secretary and office services of the outplacement office. Executives get help with counseling, resume preparation, and in many cases other information being handled in their workshop. Outplacement firms also do group work with employees at lower levels on site at the firm. These firms do not want your resume or your business. If outplacement is a part of your severance package it will be introduced to you at the time you are laid off. Some packages can cost up to $9,000.

When executives are released or dropped by organizations today, they are often referred to outplacement or career counseling consultants. These specialized consultants help them assess their skills and abilities and counsel them on how to prepare resumes and find new careers. These specialized consultants work for and are always paid by the executives, and there is often a potential conflict of interest. The Association of Executive Search Consultants (AESC) bars its members from offering outplacement services for the same reason.

Career Specialists

These are businesses that have smooth marketing programs to get you to sign a contract that you are financially responsible for anything that traffic will bear. The higher your salary the deeper they reach into your pockets (fees run from $1,000 to $5,000). I recently spoke to someone who is bitter because of all the unfulfilled promises from a career specialist. His bill was only $1,500. He is so upset that he is taking them to small claims court. Before you put your money down on one of these programs, make sure you know what you are getting. Career specialists will not place you in a new job because it is not part of the package, but it is frequently inferred.

The Executive Job Search

How Long Does It Take?

Younger executives, those at lower salary levels, and those who work in an area of science find new positions faster according to a recent study by Drake Beam Morin (a New York City career management and outplacement firm). They also average somewhat higher earnings in the new job.

The typical executive who finds himself or herself on the job market should count on at least six months to properly relocate according to the study. The average job search was 5.3 months for men and 6.0 months for women. Fortunately, many of the executives received severance pay of around six months salary which carried them through the job search process.

Age plays a major part in determining how long the job search may last. For those 25–34 years of age, the average search is 4.8 months as compared to 5.7 for 35–44 years, 6.6 for 45–54 years, and 6.9 for 55 plus years. Clearly, also, those with lower salaries also can relocate more easily. The job search averaged 5.3 months for those earning under $40,000, 5.8 for those $40,000 to $74,999, 5.7 for those $75,000 to $99,999, and 6.9 for those $100,000 plus as reported in a story in the *National Business Employment Weekly* (August 27, 1989).

How did the displaced executives find a new job? Only 4 percent said through mailings, 12 percent through a search firm, and 11 percent through advertisements. The single most used source was "network/personal contact" through which 63 percent of the men and 66 percent of the women located new positions. *Career Opportunity News*

10 Common Mistakes

1. *Failure to approach the job search as a multifaceted system* and putting too much of your effort into only one marketing method. Remember your campaign should be a mix of at least 5 of these methods.

   - personal networking

   - letters and contacts to search firms

   - answering ads

   - direct letters to companies

- regular time on research

- selective targeting

- information interviewing

2. *Failure to plan and organize your campaign.* Each week should be mapped out with time devoted to all facets of the campaign.

3. *Failure to keep thorough records of everything you do during the campaign* and particularly everyone you speak with including the date and what was discussed.

4. *Failure to maintain the "ideal job seekers attitude,"* which is to work make a friend of everyone you meet. You must put out positive energy to all people you meet during the campaign, regardless of their reaction to you. You will meet some less than charming people along the way—headhunters, executives, personnel screeners, and even people you regard as friends. Do not judge their behavior. All contacts are valuable, it's just that some are better than others. Do not try to figure out which ones are better. Many jobs have been obtained through a seemingly unimportant contact, or through a contact that seems less than friendly. Treat *everyone* with warmth and courtesy.

5. *Failure to work at maintaining positive self-esteem.* This is a tough job, but one that needs constant attention. You are a multitalented individual with much to give to this world; all you need do is put the energy into understanding that that is absolutely true. We all have more talent and ability than we ever use. Keep in touch with yours.

6. *Failure to accomplish what you planned for the day or week.* By procrastinating, wasting time or putting effort into other less productive activities you lose not only the results of those incomplete tasks, but also the motivation and momentum for the work ahead.

7. *Failure to spend enough time on the telephone.* Productivity in your campaign will be directly related to the number of calls you make per day.

8. *Failure to prepare ahead of time for an interview.* Most people do not spend enough time preparing for interviews; by doing so you will stand out. Read the section on interviewing in this book at *regular* intervals.

9. *Failure to maintain your vitality* by working to be *mentally* and *physically* fit. This is a job to be given some consideration—your campaign should include a good combination of work, rest, relaxation, exercise, and play.

10. *Failure to maintain good grooming and personal appearance* even when dressed informally (when not meeting people). Your shoes tell much about yourself. First impressions are hard to change.

Again, it is imperative that you utilize and document all possible contact and employment sources, until you determine which ones will pay the greatest dividends for you based upon your background and objectives. Do not leave any stone unturned! Keep in mind that in order to have a situation to turn down you must create one. It is possible to make positive contacts in any organization that you want!

CHAPTER 9

Time Management

Scheduling for Effectiveness

As you begin implementing the contact procedure and preparing to interview, you must start to plan and utilize your time effectively.

It is important that you have somewhere to go during each work day while you're unemployed. This means organizing and scheduling your time in a positive and meaningful fashion. Since you may no longer have an office to go to, you may tend to sit around your house. It is imperative that you not do so. For ultimate peace of mind and productive effort pick an outside "office."

In addition to the standard and probably more productive sources of prospective employment, you should generate listings of other possible contact companies by geographic location (e.g., by industrial parks, etc.). Develop a schedule for each week that will allow you to visit several secondary sourcing companies and at a minimum leave your resume and or complete an employment application form in the personnel department. Perhaps you may even be able to generate an initial interview.

Although this process should not be primary, but merely supportive, it can turn out to be very important. It may develop direct sources of employment or contacts, be a positive factor for your "mental health" and that of your family and most of all, generate a greater degree of discipline and organization in your job search program.

Schedule each week on the previous Friday. Don't be concerned with the fact that you're not expected at these "appointments." After awhile, as real interviews develop, you will have to make changes to your schedule. It's a good feeling to have somewhere to go, and right now you need all the pluses you can generate.

Schedule all of your other noncontact job-search-related activities (i.e., follow-up letters, study of materials, etc.) for the evening hours. Be certain to devote the prime-time hours to sourcing out prospective employers. Time is money, use it well!

Guidelines for Saving Time in the Job-Search Process

Keep the following guidelines in mind as you plan your search in the most efficient and meaningful fashion possible.

Good time management involves an awareness that is all we ever have to work with. We may not waste time; however, we may not use it properly. Here are some useful general tips that can be applied to your search process.

Plan

Start each day with a list of items you wish to accomplish. Do the most unpleasant tasks first. You will get a feeling of accomplishment to carry through the rest of the day.

Concentrate

Apply uninterrupted time to a project. Work on one task at a time. Remember, you can think of only one thing at a time.

Avoid Clutter

Clutter hinders concentration and can create a "snowed under" feeling. Put the highest priority item in the center of your desk and put aside all the other items.

Don't Be a Perfectionist

Strive for excellence, not only for perfection. Do 100 percent of your tasks 80 percent effectively, rather than 80 percent of your tasks 100 percent effectively.

Say No

Learn to decline, tactfully but firmly, requests that do not contribute to your tasks and goals.

Take Breaks

Relax. Long periods of work without taking a break can decrease energy, and increase boredom and physical stress. Switching from a mental task to a physical task or just relaxing for a few minutes will increase efficiency.

Don't Be a Workaholic

Don't let work interfere with the really important things in life, such as family and friends.

Preparing for Job Interviews

It is imperative that you are well prepared for all interviews. This preparation should include a knowledge of the position in question. The information may come from a search organization, networking, personal contact, or perhaps directly from the prospective employer. Do not make a negative prejudgment about an opportunity because the title and/or the general responsibilities do not sound attractive. Give yourself and the prospective employer the benefit of the doubt by visiting with him or her prior to drawing any conclusions.

It is also important to gather as much information as possible about the organization that you will be interviewing. This data can be gathered through recruiting brochures, annual reports, business publications, trade journals, feedback from present or past employers, and so on. You can make a positive impression on a prospective employer by taking the time to do some homework prior to the interview. This demonstrates a high degree of professionalism and will have a positive effect on your candidacy. It also has meaningful ego impact on the interviewer who may be impressed by the fact that you have taken the time to learn about his or her company.

Information is power. The more you are prepared, the more confidence you will have going into the interview. If you read the material supplied to you in preparation for the interview, then you are doing the minimum. If you do additional research and get information that is not given to you and introduce it into the interview, then it will have a powerful impact on your interview. If the contact person doesn't send out literature then call and ask the secretary for company materials. Another source of information is the periodical research department at a major library. Another source is a clipping service that will have all clippings that have appeared in major publications over the past several years. Some employers are too small to have glossy material but they will surely have something they can pass along to you.

Recently the introduction of CD-ROM systems has introduced a technology that makes corporate research significantly easier. These massive library systems can hold enormous amounts of information on a single disk. To give you an idea, the average computer hard disk might be 25 to 180 megabytes. That means in memory, the system can store 25 to 180 million bytes of information before it is overloaded. Although that is an enormous amount of data, it pales in comparison to a CD-ROM which holds half a gigabit of information—that is 500 million bytes of information. That is how whole dictionaries, encyclopedias, and the like can fit onto one small disk. This opens many opportunities to get information by going to the library and accessing a CD-ROM system or, if the programs are on-line, you can access the information by modem from your office, home, or lap top.

Guide to Library Research and Company Information

Listed below are some major sources for locating financial and other information for U.S companies and industries. The information given in these sources can vary and also conflict. Be sure to note your sources and read table notes. These sources primarily contain information about publicly held companies. Information concerning privately held companies is much more difficult to obtain, but can be found indexed in certain databases.

Electronic Databases

Compact Disclosure

Provides financial data from 10-K reports and the SEC filings for public corporations. Provides quarterly, annual, and retrospective annual financial information, in addition to management reports. Industry comparisons and key financial ratios are provided for many individual companies.

ABI Inform

An index to approximately 800 international and management periodicals. Contains full citations and abstracts. A thesaurus of subject terms is available. Updated monthly.

Business Dateline

Contains indexing and full text articles from about 180 regional, North American business magazines, newspapers, and wire services. An excellent source for locating information on small companies, new startups, and closely held firms. Thesaurus available. Updated monthly.

Corporate and Industry Research Reports

Indexes more than 100,000 reports written by securities and investment firms covering companies and industries. Full reports available in the Government Publications and Microforms Department. Updated quarterly (ceased subscription with 1992).

General Business File (Infotrac)

Contains article citations and some abstracts from 800 business journals and newspapers, including the *Wall Street Journal*, and the *New York Times*. Directory listings for over 100,000 companies, over 90,000 of which are private, and a database of company and industry analyst reports. Updated monthly.

Selected Business Resources in Paper

Dun & Bradstreet Industry Norms and Key Business Ratios

Contains brief industry overviews, typical balance sheets and income statements, and fourteen key business ratios for a variety of U.S. industries.

Moody's Industrial Manual

Financial information on companies, including background information and comparative figures. Lists largest companies.

Value Line Investment Survey

Investment information is provided for about 1,500 companies, revised quarterly. Ratios are provided for individual companies but not industries.

Standard and Poor's Industry Surveys

Covers about 69 major industries. Comparative data for industries including market shares, ratios, and sometimes projections. Good broad discussion of industries.

Analyst's Handbook (Standard and Poor's)

Provides composite per share stock information on over 90 industries. Retrospective data for 10 years. Updated frequently.

Worldscope Industrial Company Profiles

Very comprehensive (in geographical scope) source of brief financial data and business ratios. Provides 6 years of retrospective data.

Predicast's F & S Index

Indexes journal articles, including trade journals. Comprehensive in coverage, accessible by SIC code and company name.

CHAPTER

10

The Interview

Finding the Right Opening

Candidates assume, usually incorrectly, that recruiters use the interview process to select candidates for available positions. In reality the interview process is usually used to screen out unsuitable candidates. Applicants should be aware that only about 5 to 10 percent (or less) of the candidates interviewed receive job offers. You are also competing against candidates who are as highly motivated and experienced as yourself.

Applicants are usually rejected, not on the basis of technical ability or even experience, but on the intangible basis of organizational fit. Many companies, particularly large corporations, consist of a variety of divisions. These divisions are often in varying degrees of development and may serve very different management. Others are expanding rapidly. Others may be newly acquired. Differing styles of management require various types of skills, interests, and personalities. It is quite common for an applicant to be unsuited for one unit but very compatible for another. The interviewer's questions are often designed to determine what area gives the candidate the best chance of success. The interviewer will attempt to evaluate you not on what you are as much as what you are able to do with what you are.

Interviewing

After all these years, interviewing is still an art, not a science. People who have been interviewing for years admit it is a crapshoot at best. It comes down to an intangible gut feeling. Frequently void of rational logic, frequently void of successful track records. Employers can use all manners of devices to try to improve their batting averages: Personality tests, panel interviews, multi-interviews with many people. It is not unusual for the applicant to face 10 to 12 interviews for a key position, including spousal interviews, psychological testing, and stress interviews. Finally, it all comes down to the boss saying "Yes" or "No". Time will only tell if the decision at that time, for that person, for that particular job, was the right decision. In spite of all the devices, nothing has been devised that will predict 100 percent success.

Usually the test does not reach down into the core of that person and get a handle on what motivates that individual. What "stuff" is really at the core that would make the person overcome all odds, obstacles, defenses, lack of proper training, and education—to be successful in spite of everything standing in the way. In other words, it can't measure the heart of the individual. For that reason, or until that perfect test is devised, bosses will continue to make some good choices and some bad choices. Just a few right choices will return handsomely the return on the investment. Bad choices can be dismissed, but that can be expensive. Even the good choices may not work out because other employers will recognize they are good and come after them with a better offer. And, after all that, they may walk anyway.

It is a frustrating and expensive hit or miss process that both line managers and staff personnel are constantly practicing, never perfecting. Scads of training sessions are available and many are good, but it still comes down to that intangible that no one can really upgrade from an art to a science.

Most important—interviewers frequently make up their minds about the qualifications of an applicant during the first four to five minutes of the interview. First impressions can be crucial. Be prepared to create a very positive impression during the opening minutes of your interview.

Nonverbal cues during the first four to five minutes are so important that it is difficult to stress just how much of a role they play in your overall success. How you look, what you wear, your shoe shine, your personal hygiene, your smile, how you shake hands, your eye contact, your posture, your use of voice intonations, where and how you sit, how you use your hands, how you use energy level to rise and fall during the conversation—all of these nonverbal factors may be more important that the content of your answers.

Companies look for skills, experience, personality, and abilities that will fit into their organization. Technical skills are relatively easy to evaluate. Most people feel uncomfortable talking about attributes other than in generalities. It's easy to tell the interviewer you have good interpersonal skills or are a very skillful planner. We tend to understate this critical factor with the hope the interviewer can read between the lines and positively evaluate our claim.

It is important that you be able to transfer your claim of being people-oriented with specific examples. Be prepared to substantiate your claim to have good communication skills. The interviewer may ask you to prove your claim of being a leader. When possible, use real life illustrations, full examples, anecdotes, or stories when making your points. Do not use long, drawn out hard-to-follow illustrations. Keep them simple and to the point.

Your ability to anticipate the interviewer's desire for proof of your claims by immediately giving examples of your expertise is important. For example, if you claim to be people-oriented, give as an example how you trained employees during a position or enjoyed a sales position because of the constant contact with customers.

Preparation

As stated earlier, it is imperative that you prepare yourself well for every interview you take. The more prepared you are, the more confidence you will have going into the interview. **Information is power.** You need to gather as much information as possible about the organization with which you will be interviewing and the specific position for which you will be interviewing. This data can be obtained through personal research, recruiting brochures, annual reports, business publications, trade journals, feedback from present or past employees, or any number of resources. It demonstrates a high degree of motivation and professionalism and will have a positive effect on your candidacy.

Dress

Be certain that you are well-groomed and neatly attired for your interview. A good rule of thumb is to dress a little more formally than those currently working in a similar position at that particular company. And err on the side of conservatism. Men should wear suits, not sport suits, and women don't necessarily have to wear a suit but it is a safe bet. Dark grays, blues, and soft plaids with solid shirts are appropriate, leave the bright scarves and ties at home. Jewelry and make-up should also be subdued—meant only to enhance, not detract.

Mental State

Hopefully you are well-rested and relaxed. Try not to go into the interview with a sense of urgency or emotional upset. Approach every interview with a positive attitude. Review your resume and your research and rely on all the preparation you have done to help you present yourself in the best and most effective manner. Regardless of any prejudgments or preconceived notions you may have about the position or the company, be certain to say to yourself, "I want the job. I can get the job!"

A calm mental state is most important if you are to get an accurate feel for the organization and the interviewer(s). Keep in mind that most interviews will be a *two-way* exchange of information and ideas. You should be fully prepared to not only answer questions and deal with specific issues, but to ask a significant number of meaningful questions based upon your pre-interview research. Interviewers will expect that and you should be ready to oblige.

The Role of Personnel

Many interviews begin with a brief session in the personnel department. Although the personnel office is not the centerpiece of the interviewing process, they are not to be minimized. Personnel departments can become an obstacle but they are also a conduit to the right interview. The meeting with personnel may not only be an orientation process, but in some organizations a meaningful activity that can greatly influence the hiring decision. *Do not underestimate the role played by the personnel department.*

The decision to hire is never made by the personnel office alone but by the line person or the departmental committee which has registered the opening. Try to get as much information as possible from the personnel department relative to the job, and also try to learn about the personality and style of the individuals involved and the company's mission or operating philosophy. You will then be better prepared for the interviews with those individual(s) responsible for the hiring decision-making process.

Listen

An interview is a two-way conversation and your ability to listen is as important as having clear, articulate responses. Be sure to listen to the questions your interviewer asks you, and then respond to those specific questions. Let the interviewer lead the interview and follow him or her as best as you can. Add additional information only when appropriate and pertinent. A common mistake people make is to try and manipulate the conversation to suit their personal agenda. This is not an appropriate thing to do, and it is very apparent to the interviewer. Usually an interviewer will provide some time for you to discuss yourself in greater detail at a different stage in the interview—and then do so!

Many people assume that a senior person in the organization is well qualified to conduct the interview. It is always a shock to come across a vice-president who conducts a lousy interview. This just increases your challenge. It is a shock when a person in a position of influence asks either inappropriate or illegal questions. It is easy to generalize that if this is the type of person this organization has in positions of influence then I am not interested. Remember, this is just one person and does not necessarily reflect the attitudes of the whole organization. Hiring today is a decision made by a committee. Few people are prepared nor have the power to make unilateral hiring decisions.

The decision to hire is never made by personnel but by the line person or the departmental committee that has registered the opening. Personnel is in the middle. Line departments frequently attempt to circumvent the hiring process but use personnel in the processing or clerical part. Usually personnel departments screen, reject, or refer your resume.

Try to get as much information from the personnel department relative to the job, the personality and style of the individuals involved and the company's philosophy/policy. You will then be better prepared for the interviews with those individual(s) responsible for the hiring decision-making process.

The Sale

During your interviews, remember that no matter how impressive your background is, it will be necessary for you to sell yourself in the most effective and professional manner possible. As the inter-view proceeds, be direct and candid. If you are not certain of something, admit it and do not introduce falsehoods into the con-versation. Find out about the position and determine whether it is comparable to the ideal job as you defined it. Try to assess the personal and management styles and capabilities of the people you would be working for and with.

Try to meet your peers, not only the individual who will be your immediate supervisor. Maintain your composure and don't overreact to any question or to the environment. Be certain not to oversell yourself, and don't try to impress an individual with irrele-vant dialogue. Be certain that you are presenting yourself as you really are. The worse possible thing that could happen would be to sell yourself as being something you're not, while the prospec-tive employer is overselling the position and/or environment. It would be most frustrating on the first day of employment to find that the individual who was hired was not the individual who was interviewed, and that the environment that really exists is not the environment that was staged during the interview process.

Documentation

After an interview is concluded be certain to document it. Note the effectiveness of your preparation, your rapport or lack thereof with the interviewer, the strengths and weaknesses of your presen-tation and the interviewers, any relevant data gathered, names of people you met, and your degree of enthusiasm for the position in question. Even if you have done poorly in an interview, you can learn from it. It is important, therefore, to analyze, evaluate and document every interview as soon as possible after its conclusion.

Follow-up

Immediately after the interview, send a short note to thank the in-dividual who coordinated and/or implemented the interview.

Thank him or her, and if appropriate, his or her associates for the courtesy of their time. *Reinforce your interest if it is real!*

The success of an interview depends on what you do prior to, during, and after it. Some things to remember are the following:

1. Know yourself—review your resume prior to the interview. Reflect on your successes and your skills.

2. Sell the *quantifiable* results of your accomplishments.

3. Demonstrate your professional growth via incremental increases in responsibility.

4. Be factual about your accomplishments.

5. Put your most positive self-image forward during the interview—don't be critical of past employers and associates.

6. Relate your accomplishments to the interview's needs and requirements.

7. Extensively research the organization and the position prior to the meeting.

8. Be a good listener.

9. Answer all questions asked.

10. Do not volunteer extraneous and potentially negative information.

11. Review all standard interview questions and techniques (role-play with spouse or friend).

12. Be certain that the next step in the process is discussed prior to closing the interview. Ask if you can follow-up with them if you don't hear back in the stated time frame.

13. Follow-up the interview(s) with appropriate correspondence.

14. Be certain to document the interview.

An Executive Explains What He Looks for When Hiring

Once in a conversation with an executive, I asked what he was looking for in hiring people. He was the first one to admit hiring is still an art not a science and that although he had certain criteria, he frequently made mistakes. And he was constantly open to a more scientific way of arriving at hiring decisions. So what were his criteria? They weren't much different from what many other people use in hiring. Regardless of what position people are hiring for (proven management talent or potential management), there are three characteristics to look for in applicants. Because his business requires analytical abilities, this executive looks for people with strong proven technical skills developed through education or experience. He has to have people capable of crunching the numbers, using the computer business tools of word processing and popular spreadsheets. Even if they don't use it every day he expects the software packages to be a part of their portfolio. In addition, he looks for people with strong interpersonal skills. He has to have people with proven marketing abilities, selling to and dealing with the customer. Even if the person is not directly responsible for selling, he still wants the skill.

The way he underscored these two skills was this. We were in a high rise glass office, he looked out the window off to his left and said, "See Joe over there? That guy is great on crunching numbers. He is very analytical, capable of working on the terminal all day long. He sits at his terminal and can make Lotus sing for him. We can't get him out of the office to call on customers, he doesn't do the other part of his job but he sure is comfortable analyzing the numbers."

He then looked off to his right to another glassed-in office and said, "See Margaret. She is a great schmoozer. Everybody loves her. She is always out calling on customers. She is truly liked by all her customers. We can't get her to do the analysis, finish her projects, put together her proposals, or work the spreadsheets. But she sure is good with potential customers."

He then said, "We are looking for people who inherently have both skills but also, equally important, have a third and maybe the most important intangible characteristic—fire in the belly. I looked at him puzzled and finally asked what he meant by fire in the belly. He said you can define it anyway you like. When I pursued it, this is what he said: "I am looking for Type A people—people who are motivated by success, passion for their work, given to success, near workaholics, goal oriented, motivated internally to do the best job possible." He then proceeded to say too many people he interviews these days are Type B people—particularly the young people or current generation of early career people. These people work hard during their 40 or 50 hours but then walk off the job before the job is done. The work will be there tomorrow and they will be back tomorrow to continue. This drives him nuts. He believes in a personal life and going to the beach, but that is what Sunday afternoon is for. You don't walk out if the project isn't done. If it takes staying to 10:00 P.M., you stay. He truly believes the work ethics have eroded over the past 10 years. Now he admits you don't do that every night but when it needs to be done you get the job done!

Now how do you hire a person with the combination of analytical skills, interpersonal skills, and fire in the belly? If you ask people whether they have these three qualities they would say yes. But when you ask them to substantiate their claim, they will begin to pull out of their memory examples. From those examples a composite picture begins to form. You see, if your modus operandi includes these developed skills they are automatic, you cannot do otherwise. They are just a part of you. The boss doesn't have to tell you to stay late, you tell him you will stay and get the job done.

A question I frequently get asked is "What do you look for in hiring applicants?" If I were to single out the major problem applicants have in marketing themselves it would be passivity in the interview. So many applicants think the employer should be able to see what a great job they have done from their resume. It is rare to find an enthusiastic, but not aggressive, applicant—one with personal sales presentation, but not pushy; one with a high energy level, but not invading spatial territory; one who resonates to something said in the interview, but does not interrupt; one who smiles and is poised, but not phony and insincere; one who has done extensive research on the industry, company, and job, but does major research on minor points of the financial statement.

Focusing on Company Needs

There is a concept that is called needs-benefits linkup. It's a wonderful way to look at an interview. The idea is that the company has a need, and you provide a solution to that need. You bring your skills to that situation. And you provide a benefit to the company. It forces you to look at the needs of the organization and to get your eyes off yourself. The more you can linkup with the corporate goals and strategies the more the executive will engage you in the interview. Why? Because that is where executives live, contemplate, and strategize. It is easy to draw them out with this technique.

Companies, regardless of their basic mission, are aware they must improve their operating results if they are to survive. Consequently they are receptive to employing individuals who can introduce new skills and concepts to improve the company performance. Frequently improvement comes about through improved management techniques—an area particularly suitable to MBAs.

Developing your interview skills to accommodate the following needs can increase your chances to become the successful candidate.

- Operating systems will become more flexible, simpler, and of shorter duration. This requires fewer management levels, less employees who are more highly motivated, and greater use of teams.

- Introduction of quality improvements throughout the entire organization, not just manufacturing or quality assurance, will lead to more and continuous training.

- Compensation systems will become more flexible, and rewards will be based on team performance rather than individuals. Employment stability and job security will grow in importance.

- Greater involvement of employees in identifying and solving business problems will lead to meaningful communications and programs to enhance employee loyalty. Commitment will enhance the ability of the company to survive.

- Long-term results will grow in importance. This will require new concepts to balance this need against the traditional short-term emphasis of the typical U.S. business.

There have been thousands of words written relative to the interview process, but you will find that in any discussion between two individuals there can be no set standards, rules, or guaranteed results. Remember that an interview is a two-way conversation and that your ability to listen is as important as having clear, articulate responses.

Types of Interviews

There are generally four types of interviews you may encounter: screening, in-depth, multiple, and stress.

The first is the **screening** interview, which is becoming more popular because it can sift through applicants efficiently, quickly, and at a lower cost. These are frequently conducted by the personnel department or a lower level staff person. On-campus, 30-minute interviews are a form of screening interview. On-campus interviews have become so expensive that according to major Fortune 500 employers, the cost of a single interview now runs $120. If an organization comes to campus and interviews 10 people, that is a $1,200 investment in that school. Frequently, the employer may have 3, 4, or 5 schedules with 10 people on each schedule. If through the screening process they can take 2 to 4 people for second interviews, that is considered a good day. For this reason, major employers have been downsizing the number of campuses they recruit on to save costs. That $120 includes many things and is accounted for in many different ways (i.e., direct cost, travel expenses, advertising, etc.). The cost also covers indirect key executive time, multiple plant or home office expenses, and relocation expenses. Hiring costs include all expenses up to the time the person begins the first day on the job.

The shorter the screening interview, the more efficient for the employer, and for that reason some interviews are over before they start. The interviewer often makes a first impression, immediate decision that is difficult to reverse. Although these interviews are much less informative than other interviews, they are extremely important because if you don't pass this hurdle, there will not be another. Obviously, the most exciting interview is with a line person who speaks your language. This means someone who understands your questions and can help the conversation progress to a higher level of expertise. These people are usually guarded from first or screening interviews.

The next kind of interview is the second or **in-depth** interview. This is where it begins to get exciting. To get to this point usually means you have passed a couple of major hurdles. Your paperwork and resume have done their job and you have impressed some people. Now you may get to meet your potential boss and get down to the specifics of the potential match. In some cases, the first and second interview may come in the same afternoon. In other cases, the second interview may be set up at a later date to allow all the parties involved to give their input.

The screening interview may be conducted anywhere—on-campus, in a hotel, or in a district office—but the in-depth interview is always conducted at the place of business. It frequently may string out over multiple interviews with a number of people, or over a number of days.

The next type of interview is **multiple** interview and may be the 3rd, 4th, or 5th interview. All are considered second interviews but not the final interview. They may also include plant tours, psychological testing, luncheons, dinners, and include your spouse. These interviews may be at a ballgame or the country club with seemingly unimportant people or very important people. Usually, if the organization invests in multiple interviews, there is an 80 percent chance an offer will be forthcoming. But don't relax yet, because they haven't made their final decision. Obviously the more interviews you have the better your chances are of getting an offer.

A few years ago, one of my students passed his first screening interview in Boston and was invited back to Detroit for a position in a major consulting firm. The company interviewed him 12 hours on Saturday and 8 hours on Sunday in many different settings then sent him back to Boston. Two weeks later he and his spouse were flown out for an additional 8 hour interview including looking at housing in the suburbs. The following week he got a great surprise. A "Dear John" letter. When I confronted the employer, their response was that their only product was their people and service. Their employees have to work long hours under significant pressure and all that interviewing was designed to stress him out to see if he could handle it. Some of the committee thought he cracked under the pressure, so they rejected him. As it turned out, this student took another very good job, and in less than five years he was president and CEO of a $30 million corporation. They missed their bet!

One of the most intriguing interviews is the **stress** interview. Certainly the interview just described would qualify as a stress interview. Stress interviews were used more in the past than they are today. Although still in use, thankfully they are disappearing. The thing to remember is that stress interviews are a technique to measure not your answers but rather how you process the questions. They are designed to provoke you—to see if you will respond emotionally or lose your cool. The stress is intentional, so you should be intentional—take time in forming your responses, recognize what they are doing, and don't give them the satisfaction of winning in this game. Remember that the content of your answer is secondary. The best strategy to use in a stress interview is to smile, pause, and respond to the question without becoming defensive or resistant. Defensiveness is counterproductive, because all the other parts of the interview are to make you feel open, sharing, and relaxed. The stress interview is the opposite and creates the wrong tone for the rest of the interview.

Do not feel that you must answer demeaning, discriminating, or inappropriate questions. Rechannel the discussion to a more positive direction. You always have the final recourse. You can get up and leave the interview. Or, you can say something like *"If the purpose of this is to see if I can deal with aggressive situations, the answer is yes. I have all my life. But if you feel you must ask demeaning questions to test me, then I can assure you don't."* Usually the interviewer will drop the technique and go onto something more positive.

Following are some examples of stress situations.

- Why should I hire you? I have a whole line of people more qualified than you.

- Why would you choose to go to such an obviously inferior school?

- Send a fountain pen sliding across the table and say, *"Sell me this pen."*

- Three people sitting in a triangle with you in the middle banging questions at you.

- Inviting you into a room to sit down where there are no chairs.

- Would you sleep with your boss if it meant getting a promotion?

- Whatever your answer is the interviewer states, *"You seem to be missing the point of my question."*

- Are you willing to work 60 to 90 hour weeks, travel 50 to 60 percent of the time, and put in weekends? (This is a tricky one because you don't know if it is an honest question or a stress question. So the best answer is to break the question up and ask for amplification before answering.)

Usually answering a question with a question is not a good idea, but with stress questions sometimes it is a good idea if you are sure it is a stress question. Each of the above stress questions are actual questions encountered by people I know.

The Five Components of an Interview

It takes an average of eight interviews to land one job offer. Ideally you should have two or three offers to consider when it comes time to make a final decision. If this is the case, it will mean you have to set up 16 to 24 employment interviews along the way.

It is useful to take interviews even if the organization or job does not land on the top of your hit parade. This will accomplish two things: (1) it will give you practice swings to help refine your skills so when the really hot job comes along, your interviewing skills will be fine tuned. Play the hand out. You can always get the job offer, consider it carefully, then turn it down. (2) Until you see the interview all the way through you will not really know all the facts to make your decision. More than one person has started into an interview with reservations only to find out the content of the job had more meat to it than originally anticipated. Also, as the interview progresses you can attempt to redefine aspects of the job, suggest expanded responsibilities, or have a hand in structuring a new position. Obviously, if the job holds no interest at all for you don't waste your time or the employer's time.

It is important to remember the interview begins at first sight. Eye contact, hand shake, and appearance are all lasting impressions. As the saying goes, "You never have a second chance to make a first impression."

The first official part of the interview begins with the *ice breaker*. This is the time for small talk and greetings. A good interviewer will attempt to put you at ease in a natural, friendly way that is genuine. A cold stiff atmosphere will cripple the rest of the interview. Hopefully, he or she has read your resume and will zero in on the personal part of your resume. *"Oh, I see you are into rock climbing. How did you get started in that?"* Only about 5 percent of the interview is devoted to the ice breaker, but it should help in talking about something of which you can converse easily. Recognize that the interviewer will need to shift the conversation to the business at hand, so take care to answer questions but don't belabor any of the points. A good interviewer is one who gets you to do 80 percent of the talking; one who phrases questions so they are thought provoking and can't be answered with a yes or no. A weak interviewer is one who dominates the conversation, talks about his or her own career, or goes off on a tangent. When you run into one of these, it is difficult to wrestle away the conversation to get back on track.

Once the conversation appears to be flowing smoothly, the interviewer will move to the second part of the interview, the **probe**. This can take many forms: *"Tell me about why you went to the college you did." "What do you know about this job and about this company?" "Tell me about yourself."* The latter is one of the most feared questions, because you don't know what the interviewer is looking for, how long to make the answer, how far to go back and so on. But it is amazing how often this question comes up. The best way to handle this question is by preparing a 2 minute answer beforehand which is a summary of your life. It should include a brief statement about yourself, your early work experiences, your more recent work experience, and finally your current status. A statement like this is hard to prepare and should go through many drafts and rehearsals with a spouse or a friend.

The interviewer will set the tone, pace, mood, and depth of the interview. Frequently, first interviews are more surface and do not probe as deeply as subsequent interviews. It is a key to remember that the interview is a mutual exchange. Their goal is to get information about you and your goal is to get information about the job and the company. The interviewer measures you on a number of fronts.

- Your job specific expertise.

- Personal chemistry—how you would fit into the organization.

- Your genuine interest in this opportunity.

- You as a person. Your attitudes, behavior, intelligence, and communication skills.

- Your modus operandi on the job, your adaptability, productivity, motivation, standards of perfection, perseverance, work ethics, commitment, and so on.

- Your environment. What are the external pressures on your life? What are your family responsibilities? What is the length of commute? Are you willing to work long hours or weekends? What are your leisure time activities?

- Your style. Are you a team player, loner, committee person, entrepreneur, intellectual, or one of the boys?

- Your adjustments. What is your self-image? How do you feel about yourself? Are you adjusting to the circumstances surrounding your life?

- Your ambition. Your goals. Are you going to leave if promotions don't come fast enough? Are you an opportunist?

And finally,

- What it would take to get you into the organization. Is the pay comfortable? Are the fringe benefits sufficient? Is the package attractive or are you just too far apart to come to a satisfactory closure?

You are getting graded on many fronts simultaneously. Since it is impossible to determine which of these areas are most important to this person, the best approach is to be yourself, be honest, and be forthright. Do not try to out-guess or anticipate what the interviewer is really looking for. A professional interviewer will not give you any feedback or clues throughout the interview. He or she will not put you down, nor offer any strong encouragement. You leave the interview puzzled on how you did.

The next part of the interview is **company information**. In order for you to evaluate your interest in this job you need to have details regarding both the company in general and, more specifically, the job under consideration. This is a very important part of the interview and requires good listening skills. Listen to points that you can refer back to later, connections to tie your background into the duties and responsibilities. Look for something you can get excited about to raise your energy level in the interview. *"Mr. Brown, I heard you say a few moments ago that you anticipate a future expansion that may influence the composition of this department. That's exciting as I have had experience in a company that went from 60 professionals to 194 over a six-month period, and I had the opportunity to implement new training and systems."*

If at all possible, keep the conversation focused on the specific job for which you are interviewing or the overall objectives of the organization. One of the best techniques to be a hit in the interview is to learn beforehand where the organization is going and what its 5-year strategic plan is, then relate on that basis. This approach shows several things. First, it shows you have done outside research and second, you can bet the key executives spend a lot of time, energy, and thought on this area. In other words, it is close to where they live.

The next part of the interview is probably the most important—**questions**! The reason this is so important is that it ties together the entire process. The first part of the interview is easy. Talking about yourself, especially after a few interviews, can become mechanical. I have had people tell me that if they have to explain their work history one more time they will scream! But the question session is unique because every situation is different. It is the opportunity for you to show your stuff, your thinking processes, your assimilation abilities, your ability to pick out key information about what is going on at the organization, and finally, to focus on areas in your background you want to emphasize. It can show your depth of outside preparation and your understanding of the financial reports.

In preparing questions, you want to have more than you could possibly ask. One approach poor interviewers use is to just keep asking, *"Do you have any questions?"* Most people have 3 to 4 questions thought out in advance, but what do you do if they ask for questions 6 or 8 times? You look poorly prepared if you run out of questions.

Some applicants are under such pressure to ask unique questions of every person they meet, that it becomes difficult to keep coming up with meaningful ones. Let me give you a little tip— you don't always have to use new questions. Bear in mind you may be interviewing with numerous people, some all at one time, but mostly one-on-one. If you are getting a positive response out of one of your questions, use it over and over again. You can tell whether people are just going through the motions of answering your questions, or whether they get into the question and answer. Even though you have heard the answer from someone else, it is interesting to get another perspective.

The kind of questions you get differ with the level in the organization. If you are interviewing for a junior position where they hire a large number of people into a program, the key executive can use the same questions he or she has been asking for years. In this case he or she will compare your answers to many others that have gone before you. For a middle-or upper-level position, this is not so much the practice, but the concept is used particularly if several other candidates have been interviewed for this position.

The final part of the interview is the **close**. It can take many different forms, but it all spells closure. The standard remark is "You will be hearing from us in two weeks." Don't believe them. They seldom get back to you within the time promised. There are all kinds of reasons for this so what you want to do is build in the follow-up now for a future time. *"Mr. Jones, I am looking forward to hearing from you but if I don't hear from you within two weeks is it* *all right if I contact you to get an updated status report on my can-didacy?"* They will almost always agree. What that does is give you reason to call if you don't hear from them.

If you are dealing with a research firm, you will usually get your feedback from the agency which has a tendency to "encourage you along" and keep you involved. They are liable to ply you with strong affirmation unless there is no interest in your application.

Final Hints

Don't talk about a problem in your previous work. Never talk badly about a previous employer. Be positive. Don't say, *"Gee, the weather is lousy."* Remember, the goal is to build rapport and this is accomplished by keeping on a positive plane. Your answers to questions should be brief. Don't answer more than they ask, and know when to stop talking. The interviewer can always ask addi-tional questions for clarification or amplification.

Think back on your own hiring experiences. Don't you tend to find questions that work for you then stick with them?

If your questions are not accomplishing the right response, vary them. Realize the hiring game is today a committee decision. It must be thumbs up for all involved. The top person may have more weight, but all participants are important. In other words, you have to impress them all.

Steps to Successful Interviewing

Prior to participating in an interview:

1. Thoroughly research the company and the positions in which you are interested.

2. Think about the kinds of questions you would like to ask. Write them down.

3. Be prepared for surprise questions, perhaps awkward questions. How would you prefer to deal with uncomfortable inquiries?

4. Consider how to deal with on-the-spot nervousness, for example, by breathing deeply, doing relaxation exercises, or reviewing your resume and research information.

5. Have an opening remark in mind.

6. Be prepared to discuss salary if the subject is raised. Do your best to find out what people in similar positions make.

7. Know the time and location of the interview and plan to arrive early. Be sure to get directions if needed.

8. Take a pad and pen along for any notes you may wish to make immediately *after* the interview.

9. Dress appropriately. A good rule of thumb is to dress a little more formally than those individuals working in similar positions to the one for which you are interviewing.

During the job interview itself:

1. Know the interviewer's name. You can usually get that information from the receptionist, or, if you are interviewing on campus, the career services office will have the name.

2. Shake hands warmly and firmly. Make eye contact; look the interviewer in the eye.

3. Understand that there are things about an interview that are beyond your control; the physical setting of the interviewing room, time factors, the interviewer's mood, the interviewer's skill, and so on. These factors may contribute to the interview's outcome.

4. Take time to reflect before answering questions. Try not to fill quiet time with "an, um, well"; just let there be silence until you compose your response.

5. Be aware of your nonverbal behavior—eye contact, posture, tone of voice, and so on.

6. Keep your answers concise. The interviewer will ask for more detail if desired.

7. Stress the positive points about yourself honestly and confidently.

8. Avoid putting yourself down, but be realistic about weaknesses and be prepared to discuss them.

9. Convert opinion into fact when describing yourself; "I am a very detail-oriented person, and I like to get things done."

10. Listen to yourself; avoid saying too much or too little. Let the interviewer lead the interview.

11. Ask questions when appropriate.

12. Ask what the next step will be after the interview. Make sure you leave a door open to recontact them in the future; "If I don't hear from you within two weeks could I call you?"

13. At the end of the interview, thank the recruiter for his or her time and consideration. Send a brief thank you note within the next 2 days (preferably that day!).

Just a Few More Basics:

1. *Relax* as much as you can. This is difficult advice to follow, particularly in your first few interviews, but a conscious effort to remain calm will be beneficial. Reread your resume and review your research notes to refamiliarize yourself with the information. Breathe deeply and do relaxation exercises prior to going into the interviewing room.

2. *Be yourself.* The decision to hire a colleague rests not only on the assessment of intellectual ability, but also on personality. Employers hire candidates for whom they feel some affinity and respect.

3. *Get energized.* Employers look for and are flattered by a candidate's enthusiasm about their company. Don't be afraid to display your genuine excitement about working with them. If this isn't possible, see #4.

4. *Don't set yourself up.* If you have no interest in working in Billings, Montana, don't interview for a position there. You probably will not fool the interviewer, and you might be taking an opportunity away from another deserving individual who wants to go to Billings. Besides, who needs another rejection?

5. Try to *enjoy the exchange of information* and try to *learn from each interview.* You are in a unique position to ask probing questions about a different company—perhaps a competitor— and to learn something from each encounter.

Eighteen Job Eliminators

1. Not prepared for the interview. No research preparation on company. Don't know company or industry literature.

2. Lack of self assessment. Purposes and goals ill defined.

3. Not having questions available or not asking good questions.

4. Negative attitude during interview. Putting down past employers.

5. Poor communication skills. Unable to speak good grammar or speaking with poor diction.

6. Poorly prepared resume, cover letter, or application.

7. Arrogant and conceited. Communicate that you are too good for the position.

8. No real interest in the position, the organization, or the industry. Clearly communicating that you are shopping around.

9. Evidence of little or no interest or enthusiasm, indifference, no energy, no excitement, no personality.

10. Being withdrawn, shy, subdued, or boring.

11. Lying during the interview. Grounds for immediate dismissal when discovered after you have started the job. Lying about your degree, criminal record, drug history, and so on.

12. Lack of courtesy, ill mannered, overbearing, over aggressive, rude.

13. Communicating that you are willing to do only the minimum required on the job. Lack of willingness to work the necessary hours to get the job done.

14. Unwilling to work your way up. Expect too much too soon.

15. Interested only in the best dollar. Not willing to consider a compromise.

16. Limited geographic location interest. Unwilling to relocate.

17. Lack of confidence or poise. Poor, limp handshake, poor eye contact, looking around the room instead of at the interviewer.

18. Poor personal appearance. Not professionally dressed, needs shoes shined, shabby clothes, poor personal hygiene.

Information to Have on the Employer

Industry Information:

- Clear understanding of the industry
- Relative size of firm in the industry

- Health of industry

- Potential growth for the industry in general

- Percent market share in industry

- International perspectives of industry

- Major competitors

- Current trends in the industry

Products & Services:

- Array of products or services

- Potential new markets, products, or services

- Various price points in product or service line

Corporate Information:

- Corporate history

- Ownership/public or private company

- Familiarity with the board of directors

- Size of company

- Corporate philosophy/culture

- Organization structure—by product line, function, etc.

- Geographic locations, national and international

- Location of home office

Financial Information:

- Percent of annual sales growth for the last five years

- Percent of annual growth in earnings

- Present price of stock

- Dun & Bradstreet credit rating and financial state

- Short-term profit picture

- If a public company, recent reports on stockbrokers positions relative to company

- Structure of assets

General Information:

- Formal versus on-the-job training—is there a formal rotational program for training?

- Recent items in the news

- Names and positions of people you know in the firm

- Typical career path in your field of interest (where you might be/want to be 5 years in the future with this firm)

- Name of recruiter

Job Interview Questions

Walter R. Mahler in his book *How Effective Executives Interview* (New Jersey: Mahler Publishing Co., 1993) offers the following job interview questions.

1. Beginning with your move into your first supervisory job, would you tell me briefly why each change was made?

2. Referring to your most recent position, what would you say are some of your more important accomplishments? I'd be

interested in operating results and any other accomplishments you consider important.

3. Considering these accomplishments, what are some of the reasons for your success?

4. Were there any unusual difficulties you had to overcome in making these accomplishments?

5. What two or three things do you feel you have learned on this job?

6. What did you particularly like about the position?

7. There are always a few negatives about a position. What would you say you liked least about the position?

8. What responsibilities or results have not come up to your expectations? I'd be interested in things you had hoped and planned to accomplish which were not done.

9. What are some of the reasons for this?

10. I'm interested in how you do your planning. What planning processes have you found useful, and how do you go about them?

11. In what way do you feel you have improved in your planning in the last few years?

12. What are some examples of important types of decisions or recommendations you are called upon to make?

13. Would you describe how you went about making these types of decisions or recommendations? With whom did you talk, and so forth?

14. What decisions are easiest for you to make and which ones are more difficult?

15. Most of us can think of an important decision that we would make quite differently if we made it again. Any examples from your experience?

16. Most of us improve in our decision-making ability as we get greater experience. In what respects do you feel you have improved in your decision making?

17. What has been your experience with major expansion or reduction of force?

18. How many immediate subordinates have you selected in the past two years? How did you go about it? Any surprises or disappointments?

19. How many immediate subordinates have you removed from their jobs in the last few years? Any contemplated? One example of how you went about it.

20. How do you feel your subordinates would describe you as a delegator? Any deliberate tactics to use?

21. Some managers keep a very close check on their organization. Others use a loose rein. What pattern do you follow? How has it changed in the last few years?

22. Let's talk about standards of performance. How would you describe your own? What would your subordinates say? What would your boss say?

23. What things do you think contribute to your effectiveness as a manager?

24. From an opposite viewpoint, what do you think might interfere with your effectiveness as a manager?

25. In what respects do you feel you have improved most as a manager during the last few years?

26. What kind of supervisor gets the best performance out of you?

27. Some managers are quite deliberate about such things as communications, development, and motivation. Do you have any examples of how you do this?

28. What have you done about your own development in the last few years?

29. Some people are short-fused and impatient in their reactions. How would you describe yourself?

30. Have you encountered any health problems? What do you do about your health?

31. How do you feel about your progress (career-wise) to date?

32. What are your aspirations for the future? Have these changed?

33. Are there any conditions of personal business, health, or family which would limit your flexibility for taking on a new assignment?

Evaluation by Interviewer

One of the ways to understanding the interviewing process is to look at it from the other side of the desk. How is the employer thinking? Many of you have been in the position of hiring people into the organization. However, a review of what employers look for might be useful.

Teamwork

1. Does the candidate seem to have operated successfully as a member of a team in connection with community activities in the neighborhood, or group activities on the job?

2. Is the candidate strongly motivated to be the star of the team, taking more than his or her share of credit for accomplishments?

3. Does the candidate seem to place the accomplishments of the group ahead of his or her personal feelings and ambitions?

4. Does the candidate have the degree of tact and social sensitivity necessary for the establishment and maintenance of good interpersonal relations with other members of a team?

5. Does the candidate show any pronounced tendency to be inflexible, intolerant, or opinionated?

Follow-Through

6. Has the candidate changed jobs too frequently?

7. Once the candidate starts a job, does he or she continue with it until it has been completed, resisting any tendency to become distracted?

8. Has the candidate completed an appreciable portion of his or her college education by going to school at night?

9. Does the candidate find it inordinately difficult to complete tasks on his or her own, such as correspondence courses where he or she does not have the stimulation of group effort?

10. Is there evidence to support the view that he or she starts more things than he or she can finish?

Emotional Stability, Even Temperament

11. Has the candidate shown an ability to maintain composure in the face of frustration?

12. Has the candidate been able to maintain his or her emotional balance and mental health in the face of trying personal circumstances?

Note: Be prepared to deal directly or indirectly with these during the interview. Your candidacy may be evaluated in the light of the following, as the interviewer reviews the meeting with you.

13. Is there any evidence to indicate that the candidate is a self-starter, in the sense that he or she does not have to wait to be told what to do?

14. Does the candidate seem to have fallen into a job rut; in the sense that he or she has been unwilling to extricate himself or herself from a dead-end situation?

15. Has the candidate demonstrated a willingness to depart from the status quo in order to accomplish a given task in a new and perhaps more efficient manner?

Self-Confidence

16. Was his or her confidence undermined by overly demanding parents who tended to be perfectionists?

17. Does the candidate reflect a realistic appraisal of his or her abilities and willingness to take action?

18. During the early years was the candidate unable to compete successfully with those of his or her own age in athletics or in academic affairs?

19. Does the candidate's general manner reflect poise and presence?

20. Did the candidate suffer in comparison with a brighter brother or sister?

21. Did the candidate grow up in the shadow of a very successful father?

22. Does the candidate have sufficient confidence in his or her assets to discuss shortcomings objectively?

23. Has the candidate been reluctant to take on additional job responsibilities for fear of failure?

Conscientiousness

24. Does the candidate's record on the job reflect a tendency to let things slide?

25. Is the candidate inclined upon occasion to work evenings and weekends, even though this is not actually required by the supervisor?

26. Does the candidate tend to be a clock-watcher?

27. Does the candidate have high personal standards of workmanship?

Honesty and Sincerity

28. Was the candidate's early home environment such that he or she developed good moral and ethical standards?

29. Has the candidate come clean during the interview discussion, in the sense that he or she has shown a willingness to talk about the unfavorable aspects of his or her background as well as the favorable aspects?

30. Is there any evidence to support the view that the candidate is exclusively oriented in the direction of personal gain, to the point that he or she does not develop strong loyalties to any organization or perhaps even to his or her own family?

31. Is the candidate willing to give credit where it is due?

32. Does the candidate seem to derive satisfaction from the discussion of situations where he or she has been able to get the better of the other person or to pull a fast one?

33. Does the candidate have any appreciable tendency to exaggerate his or her own accomplishments?

34. Does the candidate's story seem to be inconsistent in terms of other selection findings, such as information developed from the application form, the preliminary interview, the aptitude tests, or the reference checks?

Maturity

35. Any tendency to rationalize the candidate's failures?

36. Has the candidate learned to accept his or her limitations and live with them?

37. Has the candidate shown:

    Chronic dissatisfaction with job duties and working conditions, reflecting an inability to take the bitter with the sweet?

    Well-formulated vocational goals?

    Responsible attitude toward his or her family?

    Over-protection and sheltering as a child?

    Effort in school confined only to those students which he or she liked?

    Good financial stability?

Adaptability

38. Has the candidate shown a liking for jobs involving contact with many types of people and diverse situations?

39. Has the candidate shown an inability to handle a number of job assignments simultaneously?

40. Has the candidate demonstrated the ability to move from one job to a completely different kind of job without undue difficulty?

41. Was the candidate raised in a provincial home atmosphere where there was relatively limited exposure to diverse situations and different types of people?

42. Does the candidate's approach to a job reflect such a tendency to be a perfectionist that he or she has to do everything just so?

Aggressiveness

43. Does the candidate's personality have considerable impact?

44. Has the candidate done a considerable amount of participation in contact sports where aggressiveness represented an important requisite?

45. Has the candidate operated successfully in the types of jobs conducive to the development of aggressiveness?

46. Is the candidate's history replete with evidence of leadership in school, on the job, or in connection with activities in the community?

47. Does the candidate tend to be introverted in the sense that he or she stays away from group activities?

Self-Discipline

48. Has the candidate shown a tendency to procrastinate unduly in carrying out the less pleasant jobs assigned to him or her?

49. Does the candidate assume his or her share of civic responsibility, even though community activities in general do not appeal to him or her?

50. Has the candidate been so conditioned by a soft, easy life that there has been relatively little need to cope with difficult problems or situations?

51. Has the candidate demonstrated a willingness to give attention to those important aspects of a job which are perhaps of less interest?

Hard Work

52. Has the candidate's history been such that he or she has become conditioned to hard work and long hours?

53. Did the candidate earn a relatively high percentage of his or her college expenses?

54. Does the candidate's general manner seem phlegmatic, reflecting a possible below-average energy level?

55. Has the candidate shown a strong dislike for overtime work?

56. Has the candidate had any experience that may have extended his or her capacity for constructive effort, such as going to school at night while carrying on a full-time job during the day?

57. Does the candidate always seem to look for the easy way out?

58. Does the candidate seem to be in excellent health, reflecting a considerable amount of vigor and stamina?

Tough-Mindedness

59. Does the candidate have a strong dislike for disciplining subordinates?

60. Is the candidate willing to take a stand for what he or she thinks is right?

61. Has the candidate demonstrated an ability to make decisions involving people who work to the disadvantage of the few but have to be made to for the good of the many?

62. Is the candidate insufficiently demanding of subordinates, in the sense that he or she is reluctant to ask them to work overtime or to push them to some extent when there is a job to be done within a certain deadline?

Sample Interview Questions— Interviewer to Candidate

Be prepared to answer questions similar to these during the interview process. Review all of them to ensure maximum preparedness. It is a good idea to note your answers in writing and, perhaps, practice them with a friend.

Preliminary

1. Tell me about yourself.

2. Would you tell me, briefly, about each position you have held since graduating from college? In each case, I'd be interested in the title of the job, how many years you were in the position, and the reason for each change.

3. As you look back on your work experience, what positions did you particularly like and what didn't you like? What specific elements and responsibilities appealed to you the most?

4. What one or two things would you say you learned from your business experience?

5. What are some of your strengths?

6. What are some of your weaknesses? How are you trying to overcome them?

Management/Control

7. Some people believe in keeping very close check over what is going on, others prefer to keep rather loose check. What is your preference?

8. What means do you use to manage your activities—how do you keep track of your responsibilities? How do you keep track of your subordinates' responsibilities?

9. What difficulties do you encounter most frequently in managing your activities?

10. Have you changed your way of maintaining control in the last few years?

11. What changes in your way of controlling might be needed if you were directing a large organization? A small one?

Development

12. What have you done in the last year to help develop your subordinates professionally? (If applicable)

13. What have you done in the last few years about your own professional development?

14. What has contributed most to your development?

15. What would you expect from a corporation in terms of professional development?

Accomplishments

16. Please describe a couple of professional accomplishments about which you are proud. Why is this significant to you? Why are these unique accomplishments in your view?

17. What would you like to accomplish in your future professional work?

18. Are there things you had hoped to accomplish but didn't? Why were they not accomplished? What would you do differently if you could do them over again?

Selection and Placement

19. I'd be interested in your experiences in recruiting and selecting personnel. What procedures did or would you follow? What difficulties were encountered? Your tricks of the trade? What do or would you look for in a candidate?

Organizational Planning and Change

20. What is the biggest change you made in the way a company was organized?

21. What are your more important convictions about what is the best organizational structure for a company?

Creativeness

22. Most of us can look back upon a new idea, a new project, or an innovation we feel proud of introducing. Please mention any you are particularly proud of. Why? What was the source of idea? What difficulties did you have to overcome?

23. Do you have any new ideas or innovations?

Supervision (if applicable)

24. As a supervisor of people, you have probably developed some convictions about what a good supervisor does. What are they?

25. As individuals take on greater responsibility, they sometimes have to *change* their way of supervision. Do you foresee any changes you might need to make if you took greater responsibility?

26. What kind of supervision tends to get optimum results from you? What do you do as a manager to get optimal results out of your subordinates?

Planning, Decision Making

27. What steps do you take to plan? How do you help your subordinates plan?

28. Think back to an important decision which was tough to make. Please describe how you worked through the decision. What differences do you see between making technical decisions and making personnel-related decisions?

29. Most of us improve on our decision-making abilities as we gain greater experience. In what aspect do you feel you have improved your decision-making techniques?

30. What decisions are the easiest for you to make and which ones are the most difficult?

31. Can you identify a decision you made which went sour? What happened to make it go sour? What did you learn from that experience?

Relationships

32. How do you manage your relationships with your peers? With your subordinates? Your supervisor?

33. What motivates you?

34. Describe your affiliations with community and/or professional groups. What are your objectives in these associations?

35. Most of us improve in our ability to relate with other people as time goes on. Have your relational skills improved? In what way? What areas would you still like to improve?

Ability to Work Under Pressure

36. Many positions require handling a number of different assignments at one time. How would you handle multiple assignments?

37. What was the heaviest pressure situation that you have faced? Describe the circumstances.

38. Under what circumstances do you get frustrated?

39. We handle some problems without any apparent strain or stress, other problems produce considerable strain or stress. What problems tend to result in more strain or stress on your part?

40. What has been the most important criticism you have received from your past supervisors?

Future

41. How do you feel about your progress (career-wise) to date? Any surprises or disappointments? What would you do if you started your career over again?

42. What are your aspirations for the future? What level of responsibility do you ultimately desire?

43. In relation to these aspirations, what do you consider your most outstanding abilities? Are those abilities going to get you where you want to go?

44. All of us have both assets and liabilities. In relation to your outstanding abilities, what do you see as some of your limitations?

Interviewing Questions

In order to evaluate job offers, candidates should have certain basic information which might not be discussed by the interviewer. In this case you should be prepared to ask some of these (or other) questions. The final decision relative to the job offer should, to some degree, be influenced by the answers to the following questions. Some of the information will be obtained through pre-interview research. Much will probably become evident during the interview. The remainder may require questioning on the part of the candidate.

Pre-interview research

1. How long has the company been in existence? Who owns it? Family dominated?

2. How long has its present management been in control?

3. What has been its gross sales and profit (or loss) pattern during the last 10 years? 5 years? 2 years?

4. Does the company have a growth plan? (see annual report)

5. What do the company's annual report and the D & B Report show about its credit rating and financial history?

6. If the company is public, what do recent stockbrokers' reports say about its management and its prospects?

7. How do the company and its products rate in its industry?

8. What is the economic trend of the industry?

Position-specific questions

9. What are the job specifications for this position?

10. Are the duties and responsibilities described clearly?

11. Is there a clear statement of the extent of authority?

12. Can the job description be altered? Upgraded?

13. Will there be opportunities for greater responsibility and broader experience?

14. How long has this position been in existence? How long has it been open?

15. Who had this position until now? Why is he or she being replaced?

16. What has happened with other people who had this position? Where did they go in the company? Outside?

17. Where does this position fit into the company's organization plan?

18. Are the reporting channels clear?

19. Is there more than one boss?

Department-specific questions

20. Does the company have any long-range plans for this department?

21. Does the department have its own budget?

22. Who are the people with whom I will work? My immediate superior? My subordinates? My associates in related departments?

23. Who controls the budget?

24. Has this department been successful? What is its reputation in the company?

25. Is there sufficient staff to handle the work load? How is the morale of the staff?

Benefits

26. Does the company have an orientation program for new employees?

27. How do I become familiar with the company policies, practices, and etiquette?

28. Does the company have a management development program? Other training programs? Where are its facilities? What resources does it utilize?

29. Does the company sponsor courses at universities, management associations, or industry conferences?

30. Does the company offer stock options or deferred payment plans? Bonus arrangement? What is the executive package at top levels?

31. Does the company have an Employee Benefits Plan (medical, life insurance, retirement)?

32. Does the company reimburse moving expenses? Losses incurred in selling one's house? Living and travel expenses while employee is commuting and finding permanent housing for family?

33. Does the company arrange employment contracts?

34. What is the company's policy regarding vacations and sick leave?

35. When and how is salary usually paid?

36. What is the employee appraisal or performance review system?

37. What are the prospects for salary increases? Promotions?

CHAPTER

11

Telephone Contacts

Making The Phone Work For You

It is not unusual for people to get an anxious, queasy feeling when thinking about or actually making a job prospect call, even when the purpose of the telephone call is simply to set an appointment. These feelings of anxiety frequently inhibit applicants from executing calls as frequently as they should, making calls in a timely fashion, or being sufficiently assertive to obtain the desired results. The following guidelines and tips should help all of you who dislike phoning prospective employers or are easily bullied by that bastion of the recruiting office—the secretary!

When Is It Appropriate to Call?

Do not conduct information, referral, or actual job interviews over the telephone. In-person meetings are most successful for these purposes, because the employer can get a sense of who you are and what you have to offer.

Telephone calls can be made in order to:

- Ascertain whether an opening exists.

- Follow up on a resume you have sent.

- Find out the status of your application.

- Schedule an interview.

- Get further information about an opportunity.

- Arrange a meeting with a contact for an informational interview.

General Tips

Before you make the call, carefully consider what it is you wish to say. If you have carefully thought through the conversation, you will feel more in control of the situation. In addition, you will be less likely to be thrown off by someone who is abrupt or unresponsive.

Know what results you would like from the conversation. If you have a clear idea of what you want, you are less likely to be detoured by verbal obstacles. Being anxious enhances your desire to hang up as soon as possible even if you have not accomplished your goal. Write down what you want to achieve from the phone contact, so that it will be clear in your mind and you will be more likely to be assertive.

Have a positive attitude; if you think you will be successful, you probably will be.

When phoning, be as presentable in dress and demeanor as you would be in person.

Always identify yourself immediately.

Use your most professional, affirmative, enthusiastic, and articulate manner. If you sound tentative or like a kid asking for a privilege, it will be easier for the employer to dismiss your request. It is also crucial to be polite, personable, and reasonable or you will be dismissed as arrogant.

You can also use the telephone to talk your way into a job interview. Many an interview and job offer were secured because a candidate convinced the employer that he or she was well worth interviewing.

Knocking Down the Obstacles

If the person you need to speak with is never in the office, or you can't get beyond the secretary, call when the secretary is most likely to be out—before normal working hours, between 12:00 and 1:00 or after 5:00 P.M. The least productive time to call is before 3:00 in the afternoon, when many people are in meetings. If the employer is out, ask the secretary the best time to call back.

Secretaries are likely to say, "May I ask why you're calling?" The following are some responses:

- "I'm calling in response to a letter from Mr. Smith."

- "It is a matter that I can only discuss with him/her."

- "This is in regard to a piece of correspondence."

- "It is a matter of mutual concern."

- "We have a business matter to discuss."

- "I have sent a letter which explains my purpose and my call is expected."

How to Get the Interview
Once You Get Through to the Employer

Be prepared with a brief statement of your experience and/or education that you think will be of greatest interest to the employer. For example, *"I have significant experience in retailing and am completing my MBA in marketing this May."*

Be very specific: *"I sent my resume to you on the 12th and would like to meet with you to discuss your opportunity."*

Have in mind some specific times to suggest for a meeting: *"Would Monday or Thursday after 2:00, or Wednesday before 12:00 be convenient?"*

Telephoning work is hard work. Do it only when you are fresh. Do not do it for an extended period of time or when you are fatigued or in a negative frame of mind. You might want to get a mirror and place it on the table next to your telephone and speak to the person in the mirror. If you smile while calling, your smile will come across the phone lines!

Informational Interviewing

Because the job market is constantly changing; because thousands of new jobs are created each month; because those who know the most about a job are those who do it; your best source of information on jobs is people. You will gain your most valuable information about jobs by interviewing people.

There are many different ways to go about informational interviewing, but the greatest problem most people encounter is fear and shyness. It seems that the great majority of people are terrified when they think about approaching people they don't know (or don't know very well) and starting up a conversation about their work, their field or their employer. If you approach your contacts appropriately and ask the right questions however, virtually everyone you interview will be friendly and helpful. People love to talk about themselves and they generally feel good about helping out another individual. You must, however, find the courage to take the initial step.

The biggest problem in informational interviews is getting them. Unless someone is making the introduction for you, it is difficult to get people to take the time out of their busy schedules.

But informational interviews take place in many places outside the office.

It is very important to make it clear at the beginning of your interview that *you are not asking for a job*; you are merely looking for information about jobs, about their field of expertise, or their company. Put your contacts at ease, let them off the hook and make sure they know you do not expect them to give you a job.

You need to treat the informational interview as a real interview in terms of your preparedness and professionalism (you are, after all, asking the contacts to spare some valuable time). You need to have researched their company and have some understanding of the position they hold (though that will probably be clarified in the interview). You also should have some idea of what types of positions you might want in that company if the opportunity presented itself. You need to have a list of questions to help you obtain the information you desire and to keep conversation flowing comfortably. You need to review your own qualifications in the event that you are asked to answer questions about yourself. The more effective you are in preparing yourself, the more positive an impression you will make. *This cannot be overemphasized*—these informational interviews are essential in an effective job search and your first impression to all contacts is *critical*.

When you ask for information and advice, not a job, you take the pressure off the person you are interviewing. You may interview in order to find out what a particular job is like, or to find out where a particular job is done. Here are some sample questions.

- How long have you worked in this job?

- What are your major responsibilities?

- How is your performance evaluated?

- What is your supervisor's job title?

- What are the major frustrations of this job?

- What job in this organization would you prefer to your own?

- What is the next step for you in your career progression in this company?

- What advice would you give to someone who wanted to do a job like yours?

- Who else do you know who would be able and willing to talk to me about this type of work?

In interviewing, as in all else, being polite is a prerequisite. Dealing with people appropriately and politely will bring many rewards. Be sure to contact the referrals your contact person has provided you in the event that he or she follows up with them. And be sure to thank the individual for his or her time. *Send a thank you note a day or two later.*

Negotiating An Offer

Achieving the Terms You Want

If a resume's purpose is to secure an interview and if the interview is the most important event in the process of finding a new job, negotiating an offer can be the most delicate. There comes a time in your search when you realize that a prospective employer is serious about wanting to hire you. In spite of the fact that the term *negotiate* has come to imply an adversarial relationship, negotiating actually means reaching an appropriate agreement with another party through discussion and conferring. It begins at the first interview and continues until either a deal is struck or terminated. From the very beginning, both parties are giving and registering information concerning their needs and desires relative to the position in question. Successful job negotiations depend on a foundation of trust. The best scenario is where both parties win.

Few people realize it, but the most important thing you can negotiate is not a dollar figure. Far more important is the nature of the job itself. Once the responsibility and budget associated with a job have been determined, then a given salary range will be indicated. If you can shape the job to your liking, then it is likely you will have less difficulty in negotiating a suitable dollar figure.

By definition, a job is simply a group of duties and responsibilities assigned to an individual who is expected to achieve certain goals. In any active, progressive organization, those duties and responsibilities will seldom stay exactly the same for any length of time. In fact, they may even change every day.

Although it is perceived that the employer holds all the cards and the interviewee is the victim, this is not true at all. A survey conducted by Heidrick & Struggles, a major executive search firm, found that key human resource executives consider building and keeping a qualified work force to be the second most critical issue they face in the '90s. The average cost of each executive turnover incident is $18,000. So it is in the interest of the employer to make sure you are the best fit. If not, better to find out now rather than 6 months down the road.

Normally, money follows content. Most jobs pay according to a professionally developed job classification and salary scale prepared in conjunction with outside consulting organizations. If the job pays $90,000, then the content, level, and reporting will be at that level. If you are making $90,000 then the employer will *perceive* your worth to be in that area. He or she would not consider you for a $150,000 job because the feeling is you would be in over your head. Now we know that is not necessarily correct but it is a common perception. Unfortunately this perception works against people who have intentionally chosen to work in fields that underpay such as education, nonprofit, government, or ministry. This stresses the importance salary plays in setting your water mark. It also stresses the importance of not rushing to take an underemployed job that is underpaid, because once you do it is hard to pull yourself back up. Better to wait and continue to search for another couple of months to get your established worth in the marketplace.

In the planning phase you should determine the bottom line salary you are willing to accept. At what point does it make sense for you not to work? Settle on a figure in your mind that you would be comfortable with regardless of the company or industry. In most cases, it would be more than you were earning before, but sometimes it is necessary to take a step downward in salary to take three steps forward, particularly if you are changing industries. In the '90s, lateral moves for the same money are not only taking place but are frequently welcomed.

All jobs are described by title, duties, salary range, and responsibilities. Most offers are quoted in mid-salary range. The difficulty is not knowing for sure where in the range this job falls. You can assume there is negotiating room (and there usually is), but you don't know how much you can negotiate before you reach the ceiling. It is a rare case when the employer will exceed the maximum range or change the job classification to accommodate an applicant (there is just too much involved such as approvals, new job descriptions, etc.). Furthermore, if you are at the top of the scale, you are faced with two problems: (1) There is no place to go at salary review time; and (2) it places a lot of attention on you. The bosses will expect exceptional performance because they are paying top dollar, and you had better be better than the others.

In some cases you may be prepared to work for considerably less than your previous employer, but usually it is not good personnel policy for an employer to hire you if there is a major discrepancy in your salary. After the newness of the job wears off or at your salary review you become discouraged believing you will never get back to where you were before. "I am making less now than I was nine years ago." "I'll never get back to where I was."

I once dealt with a person who found the ideal job, industry, and growth potential utilizing his unique skills after a long search. The problem he had was that his previous job earnings were in excess of $100,000 and the new employer was an Asian firm where *all* new hires must come in at entry-level positions starting at $25,000. No exceptions! He seriously considered the offer because it was so ideal, but ultimately turned it down. The gap was too great and living in California these days on $25,000 would be virtually impossible. In another case, I introduced a person who was making $125,000 to a job opportunity that paid $100,000. He was insulted and said he could never work for that. After all, he had a kid in college and couldn't afford the cut!

Usually, if the organization makes you an offer it is a bidding game. They now want to hire you and won't let you go for a few thousand dollars. On the other hand you should never reject an offer over a few thousand dollars if it meets your minimum requirements. Negotiate upwards.

In some cases you may not be able to negotiate more money because their practice is to pay a certain amount and no more. Possibly you can negotiate other perks like tuition if it is not a part of their benefit package. (More about this later.)

Once an employer has come to an affirmative decision regarding your employment, you can sense when it is the time to negotiate. At this stage, be absolutely clear about what you must have and what you would like in a job. If this comes too early in the interview, you can scare the employer away. "What is wrong with this person? I don't know if I want to hire him, and he's telling me how much he wants to make." Make sure you have all the cards in negotiations before you accept employment. Once the deal is struck, you cannot ask the employer to throw in a company car or more money. All the negotiations must take place beforehand. Any attempts later smack of greed or an effort to negotiate your first raise. Negotiating is a process of compromise. One of the best ways to compromise is to be informed about all the details so that you can know what to give up if necessary.

The Importance of Timing

Good timing is crucial to good negotiating. You should always let the employer initiate the salary discussion. You should never ask the question, *"What does this job pay?"* Usually, at the beginning of the interview procedure the interviewer will determine your salary bracket. This is accomplished through questions like *"What is your salary history?"* on the application form. It is necessary for you to answer these questions in some way as the interviewer needs to know if your salary requirements are in keeping with this job. If it is too high or low, it is not worth their time or yours to begin the interviewing process. So the assumption is that you meet their salary requirements or else they would not invite you into the interview. Not answering this sensitive question risks your application ending up in the circular file.

Once again, you want to avoid salary discussion as long as possible. Push it as far back into the interviewing process as possible. Let the employer bring it up when he is ready. The time will come when he might say, "Well how much would it cost to have you join us?" Or another way they may raise the issue is to state what the job pays and then ask you if you find this agreeable. An excellent response is not to answer the question directly but rather turn it around by saying, "I think it would be helpful for me to review the major aspects of the job to make sure I understand exactly what it is you want me to do. My understanding is you are looking for someone to serve as chief financial officer, report to the executive vice-president, and manage 63 people and a $43 million budget. I would have the controller, treasury, and auditing staff report to me and would be responsible for all financial matters. Is that correct?" You have done several things with this statement. First, you make sure there is good, clear communication. Second, you both agree on the tasks. Most importantly, you have tied the entire negotiating discussion to the job itself.

The old saw is to say, "I am, of course, interested in the salary, but I am more interested in the job and its challenges. I am most interested in proving myself and if I do I am sure the money will be there." This statement links performance related job issues to financial considerations.

In all your meetings with the employer, gather as much information about them as you can. Listen carefully and look for information about their flexibility, policies, and benefits. Use your contacts to find out about their reputation and what their customers think of them. Organizations naturally put their best foot forward, but check around with their customers and contact your alumni offices to see if your school has anybody working for them. As long as you ensure confidentiality then alumni will usually give you a good honest report.

Like everything else in life, negotiations involve tradeoffs. Don't couch your wants in the form of demands, but rather as requests for their consideration. Don't get involved in protracted discussions regarding areas on which you do not agree. Move onto another topic. Perhaps later you may be able to return to that troublesome issue with a compromise suggestion that will satisfy both parties.

The best way to leverage yourself in the negotiations is by using other job offers that are paying more than this offer. "Mr. Smith, I am really interested in this opportunity but it is considerably less than my other offers are running." They are likely to ask you what other offers and for how much. In this case be honest, don't lie. But if you have other offers that are within their salary range they usually will say they can meet that.

It is always a good idea to play the hand all the way out. Persist through the interviews until an offer is granted in writing. You can always turn it down if it is not exactly what you are looking for, but the offer makes you more attractive and competitive.

Complete your interviews as thoughtfully as you can and do not accept an offer if you do not intend to take it. It is highly unethical to continue to look for a better job after accepting an offer. That's bad business, and the word gets around the industry. It is better to delay your decision if possible rather than make a hasty wrong decision. It can be tempting to accept something to get back on the payroll, but if it is not the right job for you it will show up quickly. Soon you may find yourself on the street looking again.

Sometimes there comes a time when the money runs out and you have to accept something just to remain solvent. Before this happens, you need to do the exercises on money matters found elsewhere in this book. You may find it necessary to accept something at night or part-time in order to pay bills. Be sure not to work during prime interviewing hours as your main task continues to be marketing yourself. You have to be available during working hours for interviews at the employer's request.

Negotiating Compensation

At any point in your discussions where money is mentioned, you are negotiating. You exchange your talent for a salary. Salary reflects your value. Some people believe you should not change jobs for less than a 10 to 15 percent increase. This is too arbitrary. Each situation needs to be looked at individually. The best way to determine your worth is by doing research. What are other organizations paying for this job with comparable education, years of experience, background, and so on.

The words suggested are by no means the only words that can be used. So, if you prefer other phrases, by all means use them. The important thing is for you to feel comfortable with the response you are using, and to be so thoroughly prepared that you do not have to think about what you will say in those few crucial seconds when a negotiation is in process.

"Mary, before we get started, it's important for me to know how much money you are looking for. We may as well not waste our time if it's totally out of the ball park."

The principle you should always keep in mind is: you don't have to answer the question! Instead, you can avoid a direct answer with any number of responses. Here are two examples.

"Bill, I'm glad that you are ready to discuss money. It shows your sincere interest. I don't really think we'll have a problem there. But if you don't mind, I'd like to put that off until a little bit later so I can discuss it with you more intelligently. My requirements for compensation have to do with a lot more than just a single starting figure. There is the question of incentives, chances for growth, and many other factors. Incidentally, I noticed that the job description listed previous bottom-line responsibility as a requirement. Will this job have P&L responsibility?"

OR

"I appreciate your direct and candid style. Let me be equally candid. I would not have presumed to take up your time if I did not have a fairly good idea of the range you would be willing to pay for someone with my background. You have a first-rate organization, and if we can agree that there are needs where my experience and skills fit the bill, I doubt we will have a problem agreeing on compensation.

Frankly, that's not so much of a concern to me as the more basic question, which is whether or not you have the needs that would make you want me. As a matter of fact, I read in the annual report that you expect to enter a number of new markets with your industrial laser line. Is that where the job fits in?"

Please note that in neither case was the question answered. Instead it was avoided. Not only that but after the avoidance, the conversation was steered to a different subject, that of the nature of the job itself.

You may or may not prefer the approaches cited as examples. Whether you use them or not, make sure that you do arrive at a response that follows these principles and is comfortable for you. Then rehearse it until it is firmly embedded in your mind. It's important that you not think about this when the situation occurs in an interview. By that time it should be an automatic response.

How to Get an Employer to Name a Figure First

Under normal circumstances your avoidance phrases will lead to a discussion of the job requirements and how you might fill them. Some interviewers will be more persistent, however, and some will come back to the question after you have discussed the job itself. You may get a comment such as:

"Ann, I have to agree that your experience as you describe it certainly fits many of our requirements. We might have a match here. But you know, you never did tell me what kind of money you expect to make."

You might be tempted to retort with, "How much are you offering?" The problem with that answer is that it is extremely direct, and counters a question with a question. It might annoy some interviewers. Nevertheless, it is the question you want to ask, because if you name a figure first, it may be substantially less than the employer was willing to pay.

The solution here is to remember the first principle: that you do not have to answer the question directly.

Instead, remember that when someone asks what kind of money you are looking for, you have a right to assume that they are interested in making an offer. You can turn the conversation in that direction, with comments such as:

"Oh, does that mean you are interested in making me an offer?"

OR

"Tell me, your wanting to talk money at this time, does it mean that if we reach an agreement, then we are well on the way to my receiving an offer from you?"

In effect, what you have just done with a statement like that is to qualify the actual level of interest on the part of the interviewer, and to put the entire conversation in its proper perspective.

You may expect that you will get either a positive or a negative response. It does not matter. Your reply would be the same in either event.

It should follow the principle of the U-turn, where you back away from a direct confrontation, turn the conversation in another direction, then come back with a question about the range they have in mind. You will accomplish the same thing that you would with a direct response, but you avoid the danger of arousing hostility or resentment on the part of the interviewer. Your U-turn statement might go like this:

First part: "Oh. I see. Well, for my part, I have been most interested in finding the ideal situation in terms of the challenges the job provides, the growth possibilities, and the people I will be working with."

Second part: "And it seems from our conversation that I have found that here. The job that needs to be done, the commitment you have to doing it, and my role in the overall effort all appeal to me strongly."

Third part: "And while money is important, I haven't settled on any single magic number because these other considerations are more significant. Now that you bring the subject up, though, tell me, what kind of range did you have in mind for this position?"

By using this approach, you remain gracious and friendly while still avoiding a direct answer to the question. In many instances, you will find that the reply is in fact a stated range from the employer.

In those instances where the response of the employer is still noncommittal, you may be forced to give a range yourself. If so, try to have an estimate of what the job is worth before you begin discussions. You may estimate this from what others in the company are paid, from the value of similar positions in other companies in the industry, or from an agency or recruiter.

Give a range that surrounds what you believe to be the top end of the actual range. For instance, if you estimate the range between $60,000 and $70,000, you might estimate "from the high sixties to the low seventies." At the same time, you can let them know that you are a "top-of-the-range performer."

Negotiating Techniques

What to Do When You Like The Job but Not the Salary

Countless times job seekers have been offered positions at a salary they consider unacceptable, so they simple walk away. What they don't realize is that they have walked away from what could have been an ideal opportunity. Had they been aware of the following technique, they might well have been able to keep a dialogue open and get not only the job they wanted, but also the salary. If you have been made an offer for a job you like, but the salary is too low, consider using this approach.

"John, first let me say that I am very happy you decided to make me an offer. I consider the company and this position to be of extremely high caliber, with substantial growth potential. I wish I could say yes to you immediately, but frankly, I have difficulty with the level of the starting salary. At the same time, I know that job classifications are not cast in bronze, and that they are often open to redefinition.

You and I have discussed the significance of this position, and how important it is to have a superior performer in this spot. I think we both agree that I have the credentials. If I were you, keeping in mind the importance of this position, I would be very suspicious of anyone who sits here and tells you that he can do this job well, and who still values himself at a starting salary level of only (name the figure you were offered).

Is there any way we can look at this entire matter again, with respect to the nature of the job and its responsibilities, perhaps with an eye toward upgrading content, classification, and starting salary?

For my part, I know that if you are willing to make a relatively small additional investment, I will be able to show you a handsome return. I sincerely want to work for you and I hope we can reach some adjustment. Can we take another look at it?"

With a statement such as that, given in a sincere, low-key tone, you have questioned the basis of job valuation, opened the door for redefining the job and the compensation, but at the same time reaffirmed your enthusiasm for the company and the position. Since you have little to lose because your other alternative is to simply walk away, this approach is a safe one. It has also proven effective for many job seekers.

Handling the Question of
How Much You Are Making

For the most part, you can treat this question just as you would, "How much are you looking for?" The principle is the same: avoid giving a direct answer. The two examples given earlier would also be appropriate for this question. Another response might be:

"I can appreciate why you might be concerned about that. You want to be sure that the range you have set up would be sufficient to attract someone with my capabilities. From what I know of this organization, we have no problem there. If the job is right, I believe we will work out something that is agreeable to both of us, and I fully expect that I will fall within your normal ranges. With respect to the job itself..." start to bring the conversation around to the requirements of the job and its place in the overall effort).

This approach is simple, time-tested, and effective. In most instances, you will find that you can proceed to a discussion of the job and your talents before you return to the subject of money. By that time you will have sold yourself effectively, so it would be appropriate to talk money.

The primary problem in revealing your present earnings comes about when an employer attempts to use present compensation as a basis for the salary offer. This is a common problem, and I will address it now.

What to Do When an Employer
Tries to Use Present Compensation
as a Basis for a Salary Offer

Ideally, any offer should be based on the value of the position to the organization, but in reality most employers will attempt to buy talent at the lowest possible price, and will justify their offer by comparing it to your present compensation.

This can present a significant problem if you have been under-paid in the past, or if you have developed talents that now enable you to perform at a significantly higher compensation level.

In such cases, the principle to follow is that of introducing other criteria on which to base the offer. These can include the importance of the job itself; what you would have made with a raise had you elected to stay where you were; the total package compensation you had; ranges others have mentioned when considering you; or any other relevant matter. Your comment might go like this.

"I can understand that you would consider your offer to be a fair increase over my past compensation. But I think I should explain that the very reason I am here is because my contributions had far outweighed my compensation. I knew that the type of job I could handle, one such as what you are offering, commanded a higher salary. Please remember, too, that my compensation package was (20% more than base figure). Had I remained, I would have been due for a raise, which would have increased it another 10 percent. As a matter of fact, I have also talked to other people in the course of this job search and when money has been mentioned, it has been more in the range of (name a range which is acceptable to you)."

Conclude your remarks with a request for the employer to reconsider the offer, based more on the value of the job itself, rather than past compensation. Reaffirm your interest and enthusiasm for the opportunity, the company, and the people you have met.

How to Raise the Base Salary of an Offer You Like

In a well-run job campaign, you are likely to receive offers that please you. However, as the guidelines which follow point out, no matter how pleased you are, you are normally better advised not to say yes immediately.

This is because in most instances you can negotiate for a higher base salary. In fact, employers often expect to renegotiate, and if they have gone to a great deal of trouble interviewing a number of people before making an offer to you, the chances are that they are willing to go another 10 percent if that's what it takes to make you happy.

The danger, of course, is that you might give the impression that you would be an unsatisfied employee, and that you are not really eager to join the company. The following solution is an extremely important principle:

Be enthusiastic about EVERYTHING...
except the base salary.

Whenever you wish to bring out any negative, whether it is about money or the nature of the job, you will increase your bargaining position if you are first enthusiastic. Having reassured the other party of your positivism and good intentions, you can then raise corresponding questions without running the risk of their concluding that you are really not so interested after all.

Rehearse a 30-second statement in which you tell a company how enthusiastic you are. (Don't rely on your spontaneous ability to express enthusiasm for 30 seconds when you get the offer.) Also, remember that if you rehearse for 30 seconds, when the actual offer comes, you will probably complete an enthusiastic statement in 15 seconds.

Any less than that 15- to 30-second response is dangerous. The employer may fail to appreciate your enthusiasm, and hear only the negative. Put together whatever words you like, but make sure they fill the time. Here is one version that has worked for some people.

"Phil, I can't tell you how pleased I am to receive this offer from you. As I have told you, to me this job represents almost the ideal situation. The challenge is there, the commitment of the company to meet its goals is there, and my experience is precisely what is needed to make sure that things happen as they should.

"What I'm most excited about, though, is the fact that I will be working with the kind of people I feel comfortable with. For my part, I felt a positive chemistry with all of the people I met.

"Anyone would be proud to be part of your organization, and if ever there were a day when I could say that I have made the most significant, single, positive career move in my life, this would have to be it. I feel Jane and I should go out and celebrate.

"The only aspect of the whole thing that surprised me somewhat was the level of the starting salary. I had thought you would come in just a little heavier. Can you see your way clear to another $5,000?"

The $5,000 figure is used simply as an example. Generally, you might consider naming a figure which is 10 percent of the base salary offered.

When the request is phrased in this way, the chances are minimal that the employer would withdraw the offer. When this technique has been used, it has consistently resulted either in increased offers, or in a willingness to review the compensation package in a short time. The key to your effectiveness will lie in your ability to convey your enthusiasm for the position before you ask for more money.

Telling the Truth about Present Income

When it comes to financial matters in a job hunt, there can be little doubt that some people are very imaginative fabricators. However, before you exaggerate your present earnings, you should be aware that it is quite easy for an organization to verify your true salary.

In actual practice, most firms will not seek a verification of present salary, and if you do claim higher earnings, you probably will survive. Nevertheless, if anyone in a given firm has reason to suspect your claim, they have a number of avenues open to them. Some of these are as follows:

1. They may ask to see a payroll stub from your present employer.

2. They may ask to see a copy of your last tax statement, or your W-2 form.

3. They may attempt to make a verification (after you have been hired) with your former supervisor and/or personnel department.

4. They may rely on an outside agency for an investigation of your background and earnings. (It's easy to perform an accurate check on any earnings claim.)

If you have a low salary and feel you must exaggerate to be considered, be sure to hedge in terms of an expected bonus or increase in salary. In other words, state your present salary as it is, but if you have a remote chance of shortly receiving a raise or a bonus, be sure to make that level of earnings the basis for your negotiations.

Negotiating for Maximum Salary

If you are presently employed, during the initial stages of your campaign you should maintain firm salary objectives. You will need to discipline yourself against letting people discourage you, but you should be sure to aim for what you believe you are really worth.

Obviously, if you are unemployed, or otherwise under immediate pressure to make a change, this will affect the posture you take. For most people, the following guidelines should prove of some assistance.

1. Set optimistic goals for yourself and always sell quality rather than low starting price. If you are interested in change for financial reasons, you may be looking for at least a 20 percent increase in net annual take-home pay. If you allow yourself to be talked into a 10 percent increase, you may only be fooling yourself. This is particularly significant because there are people from $20,000 through $100,000 who have been getting increases with ease. Don't sell yourself short.

2. Before you do any negotiating, you should always make sure that the employer is going to extend an offer. (Complete the sale before you try to close the deal.) Remember that your first objective is to have an employer make up his mind on hiring you. If he isn't sure about you, premature financial discussions may turn him off very quickly.

3. The finer art of negotiating requires some precise insight into the other person's alternatives, along with a knack for phrasing your needs so that they seem very reasonable. You will have to communicate your point of view or the background to your thinking before you get to the stage where you are pinned down on a number. Make it easy for the employer to have some empathy with your situation.

4. During your discussions you should focus on standard of living and short-term take home pay—as opposed to gross annual income. Also, depending on how much you are presently earning, it may be better to speak in terms of percentages rather than thousands of dollars.

5. Regardless of how excited you may be when you receive an offer, you should never accept it on the spot. Always ask for time to think it over. Then, if you want the job you should try to negotiate a better financial package.

Any good organization will never withdraw an offer just because you think you are worth more. The worst that could happen would be that they would hold firm on their original offer.

Remember, if you're looking for the maximum salary offer, you must be absolutely enthused about everything but the financial aspect. This means being completely outgoing in your excitement about the job, about your future boss, about the firm, and about the future opportunity. In short, everything but the money. Make sure that they know you'd love to start immediately.

If you do not meet with any success in your negotiations, then you can always shift from negotiations concerning the present and focus instead on futures. Here I am referring to a review after six months, a better title, an automatic increase after 12 months, and so on. These are easy things for an employer to give.

The realities of negotiating a salary during a recession are always difficult, because the employer is more inclined to state a figure and say it is not negotiable. If you object he is likely to say something like, "Are you aware of how bankers, lawyers, consultants, and so on are out there looking for work? If this salary is not satisfactory I will simply go to one of the number of alternative applicants I have interviewed for this position."

Because of inflation the whole area of salary negotiations has become more fluid. Many employers have been forced to set aside their old guidelines in order to hire attractive candidates. Still, many people allow themselves to be deceived by employers who talk about increases in gross annual dollars. From a financial standpoint, what you must be concerned with are immediate and potential opportunities for improving your standard of living. In line with this, I recommend that before accepting an offer, you calculate just what an increase means in terms of added funds on a weekly basis. This generally puts things into a more meaningful perspective.

In summary, negotiating for salary is an art with many facets. The actual negotiations are surrounded with variables that include: how badly you want the job; how badly you need the job; how long you have been out of work; your financial circumstances; your frame of mind or risk capacity; and many other variables. Remember, salary is not a motivator, it is an essential. After just a few months on the job, you won't work harder because you were able to negotiate an additional $5,000. If you accept an offer substantially below your previous salary you will always feel cheated or exploited by your new employer and that can create a resentment. Studies have shown continuous job satisfaction, challenges, and promotional opportunities are all better motivators than money once the basic needs are met. Don't let lust of money keep you from new and exciting opportunities. The trend for the past five years and into the future is for salaries to be flat or even downward. I am hiring MBAs today for the same dollar figure that was the going rate five years ago. As one executive told me, I don't need the $200,000 salary that I have grown accustomed to, I could be content with $100,000! Salary is indeed an individual matter.

Trends in Fringe Benefits

If the buzz word for the '90s is cost containment then organizations are looking at all the major cost centers to see where they can trim. One that surfaces immediately is the extraordinary increase of cost associated with delivering fringe benefits. Only a few years ago fringe benefit executives would sit around and see what nice things they could provide for their people. But today they no longer can explore these options. Instead they are taking a long hard look to see what fringe benefits they can cut.

The first one that comes to the surface is benefits tied to health. Today, 14 percent of the GNP, something like $890 billion, is associated with delivering health services by both public and private sectors. By the mid-nineties, it is expected to rise to 16 percent of GNP and will exceed a trillion dollars. Interest and health care costs are among the highest expenses in the nation.

This affects the older working force because employers can substantially reduce their cost by getting rid of those who are in the 57 to 65 age bracket and are statistically a higher risk than the younger work force. As these people are being released, the managers are discovering that what they had taken for granted over the past years is *very* expensive to pay for on their own.

Of course, all employees are eligible for Cobra but that is for a limited time of 18 months. Cobra is the continuation of your benefits with the same carrier you had through your employer before you were laid off. Instead of your employer paying the premium you are eligible for full services, but you pay the full fee. The premiums can be substantial—anywhere from bare bones coverage of $5,000 a year to $12,000 a year. The average is around $9,000 to $10,000 for the coverage most people were accustomed to as employees. What happens is people just won't pay that kind of money and that is one reason why there are 40 million people uninsured and many additional millions underemployed.

The trend of the future is for employers to give employees benefits that don't cost them anything. One example is a 9/80 plan. This is where you work 80 hours in 9 days instead of 10, by adding one hour of work to those 9 work days. The result is the 10th day off. Every other week you get a 3-day weekend. It doesn't work for everybody, but many employees think it is great. Another example is buying back vacation time. This is where you can buy an additional week's vacation time and have the cost of that week divided out over the year by payroll deduction. In some situations, additional time off is worth more than the week's pay. A third example is telecommuting. There is a growing trend toward working away from the office, thus saving commuting time, stress, and expenses a few days a week.

All of these examples are considered freebies by the organization. They don't cost the organization any money except the additional administrative cost to set up and maintain them. But they are perceived as being very valuable to employees.

A final few thoughts about the trends in fringe benefits is the talk about portability of benefits, particularly pension and 401K plans. Today, pension portability is not permitted. Pensions can't travel with people when they change employers. When a mid-level manager plans on a certain life-style based on regular contributions into a retirement plan, and that employment is terminated, this will seriously impact the bottom line of money received at retirement age. Furthermore, the new firm is likely not to include the manager in the retirement program, or the new firm may have a five-year vested scheme. At best, the person loses substantial money at retirement. Employers frequently exclude pre-existing conditions, particularly in health issues (i.e., previous breast cancer, heart operations, and a thousand other things). That can be scary for people who are relieved and delighted to be back on the payroll of a new employer again, but without the medical coverage of a major past problem which could become a future problem. None of this would be a concern if termination had never taken place in the first place.

Until recently, the compensation negotiations centered around the salary issue. Fringe benefits were automatically bestowed upon you. Over the past five years, and certainly over the next ten years, fringe benefits have and are taking on greater importance and a bigger role in the negotiations. According to the U.S. Chamber of Commerce the average cost of fringe benefits nationwide is 38 percent of corporate salaries. In a Heidrick & Struggles study, the *number one* concern of human resource managers is controlling employee benefit program costs.

There are many new and exciting compensatory arrangements employers are negotiating and are agreeing to that are not directly associated with money. The wave of the future will be in this direction as people are more concerned with the quality of life. Values and Life-style (VALS) are frequently more important than increased dollars. Benefits such as job sharing, flexitime, on-site daycare, on-site health facilities, and industrial sabbaticals are a few examples of negotiated options.

When I was at Boston University, I had the privilege of signing a chit for my two children in college. Although it was many years ago, that benefit was worth $18,000 a year. One of the benefits of working for a college is a full or partial tuition benefit. Since I have three children who will be in college at the same time, it can become the grandfather of all the other fringe benefits.

Another concept that has come of age is the cafeteria approach to fringe benefits. Instead of requiring everyone to have the same package, the employee may now make decisions on what is most important to him or her and select from a full range of options. Not all people are the same and their fringes should not be the same. To those with small children, company paid daycare may be important. To someone whose children are grown, daycare no longer holds value but maximum participation in the company's retirement program is of equal benefit. Each employee is given a percentage of salary that he or she cannot go beyond in choosing optional fringe items. How benefit packages are designed is determined by life-style.

Because fringe benefits have become such a major financial consideration, employers are balking at the huge amounts of money they have to set aside in escrow to meet company obligations and government policy. They are looking for ways for fringe benefits to become increasingly co-pay, and for ways to reduce their portion of the co-pay. They are offering many more alternatives (i.e., instead of one or two health plans maybe five or six). But the employee has various dollar contributions due to single or family plans. Some companies give you a core package that consists of bare necessities like limited health, life, dental, and so on. They allocate a percentage of your salary which is what the company contributes to your fringe benefit package. They then give you a list of services that are available. You make your choices based on your situation. If your choices add up to more than the company offers, you pay the difference out of your paycheck. This is an excellent approach to two family incomes as both spouses can make sure their fringe benefits compliment each other and are not redundant.

In many cases, these are not negotiable with a prospective employer. However, for an increasing number of enlightened firms, they are finding that they are able to attract excellent people who appreciate the flexibility. It is difficult to move from an enlightened company back to a company that force-feeds the benefit package to you. With two-income families, some spouses take employment where the fringe benefits total more than the salary.

Fringe Benefit Options

Benefits might include (but need not be limited to) the following.

Accidental death

Bonus

Company car

Company incentive program

Deferred income

Dental plan

Disability insurance

Discount purchasing

Elderly care

Employee assistance plan

Employer sponsored daycare

Employer stock ownership plan

Employment contract

Equity options

Expense account

Flexible savings accounts

Free tuition for spouses/children

Group health insurance

Group life insurance

Health coverage

Health/wellness education

HMO option

Insurance

Joining Bonus

Life insurance

Long-term disability

Long-term employment

Low cost loans

Memberships

Paid vacation

Parachutes attached

Paternity leave

Pay-for-performance incentives

Pension or annuity

Preretirement planning seminars

Prescription drug plan

Profit sharing

Relocation allowance

Sabbaticals

Short-term disability

Stock options

Tax shelters

Thrift plans

Tuition reimbursement

Vision care plans

Evaluating The Offer

Know the Value of What You Are Getting

As a job seeker, your most difficult decision may involve the evaluation of comparative offers. If you are young, or just starting out, the decision may be quite easy. My recommendation is to always put future opportunity over starting salary.

If you are an executive, there are very few rules of thumb that I can provide. However, I have found that it does help to take the time to write out the positives and negatives of comparative offers on paper. While it is always convenient if the highest salary offer is also the position with the most growth potential, things rarely, if ever, seem to work out that way.

When you decide to accept a job, you should always accept it verbally, and then confirm your acceptance in writing. The purpose of this letter is to restate the terms under which you have agreed to work for the organization. Hopefully, they will do the same.

When you receive the first offer of employment, don't feel compelled to accept it on the spot even though it might be extremely attractive. At times, the trauma of having to seek a new direction combined with any accompanying economic and psychological stress may cause an individual to accept a position that is less than desirable. You may create very severe problems for yourself and your employer by taking a position out of a sense of urgency. These problems could far exceed those of being unemployed for a while longer! If you have a definite offer in hand and the prospective employer requires a fairly immediate answer, it is not only reasonable, but courteous to contact other possible employment sources and indicate to them that you have situation(s) pending and would like feedback relative to the status of your candidacy. Keep in mind that the prospective employer who questions and/or is not responsive to this kind of delay may not be the right employer for you.

Whether you have a single or a multiple number of offers you should evaluate each one in light of the results of the exercises you have completed earlier in this book. Your decision should be well thought out and reflect all of the factors considered. In addition, the following checklist should be used to assist you in making your decision.

1. Is the job meaningful? Will it offer you the opportunity to do the things you want to do, and to get the type and level of support that you need?

2. What do you think of your prospective boss? What kind of person is he or she—Understanding, responsive, etc? What kind of match with your personality and style?

3. What about the other people in the organization, in particular those with whom you will be working? Have you met some of your colleagues? You will probably have more contact with many of them than you will with your supervisors.

4. What about the organization? What is its reputation in terms of employee relations? Its image in the industry, the job market?

5. What is the potential for upward movement in the organization? What are the organization's basic criteria for promotion? Does it promote from within?

6. What are the organization's employment policies and practices? These can be quite indicative of the personality of the organization.

7. What are the organization's compensation programs? Are they competitive in the industry? Have they profit sharing? Performance bonuses? What about the benefit plans? Are they non-contributory?

8. Have you reviewed the organization's literature (recruitment brochures, personnel manual)? Does the organization have an employee newspaper? This may be a reflection of the personality and attitude of the company.

9. How does the organization compare to others you interviewed with or are familiar with?

Choose the Right Job

Another approach to addressing the issues of importance is to consider the following job factors. Rank each of the following factors according to its importance to your job satisfaction.

1. Location

2. Good location for spouse's career

3. Travel

4. Salary

5. Benefits

6. Immediate use of training and experience

7. Learning potential

8. Significant responsibility

9. Variety of work

10. Job status

11. Independence

12. Opportunity for creativity

13. Skill transferability

14. People management opportunity

15. Asset management opportunity

16. Advancement

17. Image of company

18. Exposure to outstanding professionals

19. Quality of management

20. Industry

If an offer of employment is made to you in writing, it is appropriate for you to respond to it with a written acknowledgment of acceptance, refusal, or an explanation of the reason(s) for the delay. In certain cases, prospective employers will make a verbal offer and for a variety of reasons not confirm it in writing. There is no reason why you cannot ask for a written offer, directly or even indirectly.

Frequently, the offer will come several days later by phone or letter. It is wise for you to find out if there are any further conditions which must be met, like a physical examination or confirmation by the board of directors. Then ask for the offer to be confirmed in writing to avoid any misunderstandings. The letter of confirmation should be complete and cover all aspects of the agreement such as salary, guaranteed bonuses, car allowance, and so on. Never accept a job on the spot. Ask for at least a day to review everything and make your decision.

In any event, don't acknowledge your acceptance of any offers unless you are completely comfortable with all of the circumstances surrounding it. Be flexible, but don't put yourself, the prospective employer and perhaps even the referral source in an uncomfortable and potentially embarrassing position.

Contracts and Termination Agreements

It is very difficult to generalize about employment contracts. In recent years, many organizations have been more forceful in taking a stand against them. Their reasons for doing so are quite simple. Contracts usually guarantee employees a certain compensation for a prescribed length of time—as long as they work to the best of their abilities in normal business hours. Employers are guaranteed very little, and the individual can usually break a contract quite easily.

On the other hand, corporations are usually forced into financial settlement if they choose to dismiss an executive under contract. When arguments over broken contracts cannot be resolved, the courts most frequently rule in favor of the individual.

Despite corporate policies against contracts, it is difficult to conceive of any firm that would be willing to lose a sought-after executive simply to maintain its policy. A contract is just one additional element in the total negotiable package, as are any matters relating to salary bonuses, stock option participation, and so on.

If you can possibly arrange it, a contract will usually be to your advantage. While you can always be dropped, a contract can provide you a measure of financial security and a certain degree of independence from corporate politics.

In many cases, the mere possession of a contract may be the most significant status symbol that exists in a firm. For senior executives, a contract usually has a higher priority than amount of salary. This is especially true if a corporation is likely to experience turnover in top management, or if a firm is occasionally the subject of merger or acquisition discussions.

As a general rule, I feel that anyone above $75,000 should never be reluctant to ask for a contract. A request, as opposed to a demand, will never result in a revoked job offer, and again there is always a chance that they may agree to your request. Don't be deterred by the fact that you have heard that the firm does not give contracts. There is always a first time for everything, and as previously mentioned, if a firm really wants you, a contract request will not stand in its way.

This is not meant to imply that the contract will be won easily. You should be aware that your first request may result in a number of negatively phrased routine comments. The most common ploy is to hint that your request reflects a lack of confidence in a firm, their management, or in your own ability. They may also ask you if you are the kind of executive who values security more than opportunity. You should anticipate comments such as:

"Your contract request makes me wonder if you have the self-confidence and entrepreneurial qualities that you've indicated. We're also very concerned about your trust in us. If your relationship is going to be as successful as we all plan, I think it should begin on a note of mutual trust and integrity."

As long as you anticipate them, these types of questions should be easy to address. There is usually only one major disadvantage to you that goes along with most contracts. If you request one, your employer may insist on inserting a protective clause that would limit your ability to take future employment with a competitor.

The insertion of such a clause is often requested as a show of good faith, and is quite hard to refuse without creating serious doubt in the mind of your new employer.

If you are at an executive level, there are certain companies with whom you must be very firm in your request for a contract. These would include: companies in financial trouble; firms that are merger or acquisition candidates or those recently merged or acquired; family-controlled and private companies; and companies where one individual personally dominates the environment.

In these unstable situations you might consider seeking a three-year contract that covers your minimum compensation, and that also has provisions for such things as bonuses, deferred compensation, moving expenses, annual renegotiation upward and profit sharing.

You also may be able to negotiate life insurance, release with compensation in case of merger, salary benefits to your family in case of death, special reimbursements for foreign service, and consulting fees in the event of termination after the end of the contract period. In any event, don't treat contract terms lightly, and be sure to review all the fine print with a competent lawyer.

In recent years there has been a considerable growth in the use of termination agreements. In most cases these are substitutes for employment contracts. Termination agreements are usually in the form of a short letter in which an employer agrees to an irrevocable severance compensation. I personally favor the idea of these agreements and think that they can be designed to adequately serve the needs of most executive job candidates.

In some industries these agreements have already become quite common at salary levels of about $60,000. However, I also know of a number of instances where people earning $40,000 have been successful in negotiating termination agreements. In most cases, they provide for a minimum severance compensation of six month's salary, along with relocation and outplacement assistance, and a six-month extension of all insurance benefits.

Any agreement that you accept should explicitly cover any and all situations under which an employer may choose to terminate your services.

Parachute Options

Parachutes are usually negotiated at the time of a merger, or threat of merger, or when recruited out of a secure job (usually by an executive search firm) into a new opportunity. Companies typically do not offer parachutes to internal applicants being promoted from say senior vice-president to executive vice-president.

Parachutes are individually negotiated for maybe only the top 5 percent of key executives. It could include one-year minimum salary, possibly two or three years, and in a few rare cases could be anytime during employment.

In some cases a contract might read, "If you elect not to keep me on the job..." That is if you terminate me I will "pull the parachute," or "if you put me in a job below my skill level I will pull the chute." Parachutes are totally under the employee's control. Typically, a parachute could include:

- 1 to 2 year's vesting in a 401K or like instrument.

- Lifetime supplemental life insurance.

- Keep country club membership.

- Keep company car.

- Any number of other options or combinations.

Parachutes are different than employment contracts. Parachutes are only for the elite few. Employment contracts fit most mid-level executives. Typically, corporations laying off a work force give two week's notice with one week pay for every year of service. The higher you are in the organization the more perks, benefits, and severance packages you are entitled to, but not parachutes. The final determination is based upon many factors including how well regarded you were, what your personal family or financial situations is, how fearful the organization is of a wrongful discharge suit, and how long you have been in the organization. Organizations have learned it is good business to treat reduction in force

(RIF) people well. They will surface again either in court, as colleagues, customers, or competitors.

International Negotiations

All of my comments on contracts pertain to employment situations as they exist in the United States. If you are seeking a position out of the United States there is an entirely different environment regarding contracts. Most European nations have enacted laws that are very much in the interest of the employee. In addition, employment contracts are quite common at relatively low salary levels.

It is not unusual for a European company to give an individual two year's notice prior to terminating his or her services. At the time of severance, there may also be additional cash payments made to the individual.

Negotiations for salaries with employers outside the United States take on a whole different package. The fringe benefits frequently amount to an additional 50 percent above the domestic rate. The fringe benefits can include servants, maids, chauffeurs, and return airline tickets several times a year (all almost always tax-free).

When employers hire for international appointments, they are usually looking for long-term commitments, not just "I would like to spend two years in Switzerland." If you are interested in international employment, you need to deal with the vice-president of international operations. That person can be located through *Standard & Poor's* or *Moody's* in any major library.

CHAPTER

14

Frequently Asked Questions

Most Common Questions Candidates Ask about the Job Search Process

1. *Should I have several different types of resumes so that I can apply for different kinds of jobs?*

A multiple number of resumes obviously will allow you to give greater scope to your job search. If this is the case, I would suggest that you be very careful relative to control of distribution of your resumes so that you will not run the risk of being embarrassed when a prospective employer receives several different copies of your resume. If the resume is developed properly, it will serve a variety of situations.

2. *How do I respond when someone asks me why am I unemployed?*

The best way to handle this is in a very direct and honest fashion. A false statement may get you over the initial hurdle, but come back to haunt you in the future.

246 Frequently Asked Questions

3. *Should I answer an ad where the stated salary is considerably more than what I was making in my last job?*

As long as you can justify responding to an ad in terms of your educational background and work experience there is no reason why you cannot pursue these kinds of situations. You must keep in mind that one contact may develop another one and perhaps the organization in question might have other situations available that could prove to be attractive to you.

4. *How can I be certain that my references will give me a good reference as opposed to a weak one?*

Be certain to ask individuals who you intend to use as references for their approval before doing so. You can be certain that if anyone volunteers to act as a reference for you, they will be fully prepared to support you in every possible way. If your presentation follows the guidelines in this manual, most prospective employers will not be concerned by the fact that you may have been terminated and will look beyond this for positive factors in your candidacy.

5. *How can I convince a prospective employer to offer me a position that perhaps pays less than what I was making with my last employer? Would they not feel that I was taking a stop gap job and would leave them as soon as a better opportunity came along? This would be a major problem if I was seriously interested in the opportunity more than just the initial level of compensation!*

Many prospective employers will probably initially react negatively to any candidate who is willing to take a substantial salary decrease. However, if you take the same honest and direct approach in any dealings with prospective employers as you did with yourself during Exercises 1 and 2 and your resume preparation, then you should be able to convince the individual that you are sincerely seeking not only a job but an opportunity for future growth and contribution.

6. *How should I handle any questions relative to salary require-*
ments, especially on initial employment applications and related
documents? I don't want to put myself in a position to sell myself
short.

The best way to approach this is to indicate what your most recent level of compensation was and let the prospective employer
determine what he or she feels is an equitable level of compensation. On the other hand, you can just indicate that your salary requirements are open and negotiable. This will tell the prospective
employer that you are quite willing to be objective and flexible
about the situation.

7. *After I receive an offer, what action should I take—especially if*
it's the first offer received?

During the interview process you should make it known to
prospective employers that you are also looking at other situations. This allows you to then respond to an offer by saying that
you need some time to continue looking at your other options.
Try to be certain that you show the prospective employer that you
are quite interested in the offer.

8. *How do I respond to a request relative to pre-employment psycho-*
logical or aptitude testing?

Do not indicate to a prospective employer that you have any
fear or concern about taking any sort of psychological or aptitude
test. Perhaps you may indicate that you've never taken this kind of
test before, but would be most happy to do so if that's part of
their employment process. Also indicate that you feel this might
give you an opportunity to learn some interesting things about
yourself.

9. *What action should I take if I get no response from the employ-*
ment agency/search firm contacts that I have made?

Give each employment agency or search firm a week or so after your initial interview to process your paperwork. Then call them back and find out what their action plan is relative to your situation. Do not put yourself in a position where you do not know what the agency's next step is. Do not have any hesitancy in following up with them on a regular basis. They all have many candidates to deal with and unless you keep your candidacy unique and viable through resume format, personal presentation, and follow-up, you could get lost in the shuffle of papers.

10. *Your resume suggests that you may be overqualified or too experienced for this position. What's your opinion?*

Stress that your experience is very valuable and transferable and that the employer would get a bargain or value from your employment. Also, assuming you perform, there would be additional opportunities opening for you. Point out that experienced executives are always at a premium. Suggest that since you are so well qualified, the employer will get a fast return on his investment.

11. *Why should I hire you when we have a long line of qualified applicants who are younger, less expensive, and more recently educated?*

This question takes on many forms, but one you frequently encounter. Try this response: "Mr. Jones, there is no doubt you can find less experienced people than myself. I was once young and inexperienced but through many experiences in life and at work, you mature, your judgment sharpens, and your decisions hit the mark more often. You can hire that younger person and, someday, if they have as much experience as I have, they too would be able to make the contributions that I can make."

12. *It appears to me you have been out of work a long time.*

"Because of the recession I was caught by a company that downsized. Since this caught me by surprise I began the job search from scratch and have been successful. I have had opportunities but do not feel the right situation has come along so I would rather wait for the right career move rather than jump at a job."

13. *How do you explain gaps in your employment?*

It is your option as to when you begin your career chronology, but once you start, do not leave gaps. If there is a gap, be brief, honest, and direct.

14. *How do I handle it if I have been fired?*

Most companies today do not fire you. They will allow you to resign first. The important issue is your references. Will the company give you a good recommendation? There are several ways you can determine this. Establish a file with your college placement office. Have the reference sent to the placement office. Have the placement office screen your reference against any negative comments. This can also be done sometimes with a search organization.

15. *Does the company get written references?*

For legal reasons, many employers will get references over the phone rather than in writing. Employers are more honest and willing to cooperate. Written references can be held liable. Increasingly, companies are not giving out recommendations other than "Yes, John worked here from October 1981–June 1990."

EPILOGUE

How This Book Became Reality

While I was writing this book, it never occurred to me that I would ever lose my job. I wrote the book on behalf of the hundreds and thousands I have counseled over the years. It was a theoretical presentation—observations—but not experiential. Yes, it happened once, 25 years ago, but that was when the entire department was being shut down. Then, one ordinary day last April I was called to the boss's office. I didn't think much of it since it was budget time. So, I gathered up my charts and data to argue for next year's funds. I settled myself into his padded chair and was greeted with the surprise of my life. I was being terminated! My position, as constituted, was being eliminated. The school was going in a new direction, but I wasn't going to be a part of it.

Just that quickly I was out of my job. I inquired about causes, and the only answer I received was that two faculty people on my committee didn't like my style! My performance was not the issue. I did everything above and beyond what I was asked. But, in the changed atmosphere of my workplace, that wasn't enough.

I was asked to vacate my office in a week. I would be paid through my contract, June 30. Just that quickly I was cut loose into the worst recession in 30 years.

I immediately began to re-read this manuscript, applied the principles, and went through every phase from the pity party to discouragement, networking, and mailing resumes. The process was shorter than average, but going through it I didn't know I would be back working in four months as a Manager of College Relations for a major California bank, doing what I love to do—interviewing people.

A rainbow always comes after the storm, not before.

Bibliography

Balzar, John. "Swing Shift: The Change in U.S. Jobs." *Los Angeles Times,* April 1993.

Becker, Gary. "What Keeps Older Workers Off the Job Rolls?" *Business Week,* March 1990.

Bureau of Labor Statistics (BLS). "Unemployment: White Collar Workers Are Hit the Hardest." *Business Week,* October 1992.

Castro, Janice. "Disposable Workers." *Time,* March 1993.

Faber, Alan. "Outplacement Manual and Termination Process." Elmer J. Roka Associates.

Grant, Linda. "Fired at Fifty." *Los Angeles Times,* September 1992.

Kennedy, James. "We're Not Hiring." *The Interviewer's Edge,* 1992.

————. *Directory of Executive Recruiters.* Kennedy Publications, 1990.

Koretz, Gene. "What Happens to the Jobless? Many Don't Bounce Back." *Business Week,* September 1992.

————. "A Worker Exodus That Could Weaken Productivity." *Business Week,* July 1990.

Labich, Kenneth. "The New Unemployed." *Fortune Magazine,* March 1993.

Magnet, Myron. "Why Job Growth Is Stalled." *Fortune Magazine,* March 1993.

Roka, Elmer. "Outplacement Manual and Termination Process." Elmer J. Roka Associates.